THE HOTEL RECEPTIONIST

The Hotel Receptionist

Second Edition

Grace and Jane Paige

Chapter on Legal Aspects by Alan Pannett

HOLT, RINEHART AND WINSTON

London · New York · Sydney · Toronto

Holt, Rinehart and Winston Ltd: 1 St Anne's Road,
Eastbourne, East Sussex BN21 3UN

British Library Cataloguing in Publication Data

Paige, Grace
    The hotel receptionist. — 2nd ed
    1. Receptionists   2. Hotels, taverns, etc.
    — Employees
    I. Title   II. Paige, Jane
    647'.94   TX930

ISBN 0–03–910521–0

First published by Cassell Ltd, 1977
Second edition, 1984
Copyright © 1977 by Grace Paige.
Copyright © 1984 by Holt, Rinehart and Winston Ltd.

Printed and bound in Great Britain by
Mackays of Chatham Ltd.

Last digit is print no: 9 8 7 6 5 4 3

Preface

This latest edition of *The Hotel Receptionist* is a completely revised and updated text with new chapters highlighting the emphasis now being placed on sales and marketing.

The rapid expansion of the hotel and tourism industry during the past two decades has been phenomenal and modern microcomputer technology has revolutionised front office procedures. However, the basic principles underlying good hotel reception will still be applicable whether a hotel has the latest sophisticated computerised equipment or is manually operated.

The aim of this text is to provide a reference book covering all aspects of front office training and which is suitable for students studying for City and Guilds Hotel Reception examinations, BTEC certificates and diplomas and membership examinations of the Hotel Catering and Institutional Management Association (HCIMA).

It is also hoped that this book will provide basic information useful to any trainee in hotel management and hoteliers or others comparatively new to the industry.

Contents

1 Introduction

1.1 THE HOTEL INDUSTRY

In the ever shrinking, fast-moving world of today, boats, trains, aeroplanes and cars carry travellers all over the globe, either as tourists or in the normal course of their business. These travellers normally require food, lodging, hospitality and service of a good standard.

Progressive and enterprising caterers and hotel proprietors constantly study and analyse in detail the current trends and developments in the industry in order to provide a high standard of accommodation and service at reasonable prices and to improve the efficiency of their establishments. They are also aware of the need to make their establishments bright and cheerful with all the modern conveniences, whilst also preserving the spirit and traditions of the inns of older times.

The Hotel Proprietors Act of 1956 defines a hotel as 'an establishment offering food and drink and sleeping accommodation if so required to any traveller who appears able and willing to pay for services and facilities provided'. Therefore, by common law a hotel must offer food and accommodation to its guests; but it must also assume a liability for the property of guests, conform to public health and safety regulations, and provide a high standard of cleanliness and sanitation.

The growth and international expansion of the hotel and catering industry has been phenomenal during the past decade, ensuring a constant demand for trained and skilled staff and providing ample opportunity for those who are temperamentally suited to the industry. In Britain alone over a million people are employed in hotels, motels, guest houses and catering establishments. In America the tourist industry grosses billions of dollars a year. In Spain, Portugal, Majorca, the Canary Islands, the West Indies, American states such as Florida, and Hawaii, and many other countries, tourism is the principal industry.

1.2 DIFFERENT TYPES OF HOTELS

Hotels fall into many categories, ranging from boarding houses, guest houses, country inns, small hotels with between 25 to 50 bedrooms, medium-sized hotels with up to 200 bedrooms, large hotels with several hundred bedrooms, and special transient hotels such as motels, motorway hotels, post-houses, airport hotels and hotels in large cities whose business consists mainly of guests in transit that stay for one or two nights only.

The type of guest for which a hotel caters gives it special characteristics and atmosphere: for example, some hotels are family-type hotels with a fair proportion of residential guests, while others are commercial hotels usually catering for commercial travellers continually in transit. There are the resort hotels, which are seasonal and cater for holidaymakers, though many of these are now also providing facilities for large conferences and trade fairs, which gives them an additional form of income. Then there are the large international hotels whose operations are geared to the needs of overseas travellers.

Many orgainsations such as the AA (Automobile Association) and RAC (Royal Automobile Club) and others make their own classification of hotels and restaurants and award stars or seals of merit as guides to travellers and tourists. The classification of hotels by the AA, to mention just one, in addition to providing an indication of the type of hotel, is often regarded as an accepted mark of quality in all classifications from the simplest inn to the most luxurious hotel.

What the AA star classifications indicate

* Hotels and inns generally of small scale with acceptable facilities and furnishings. All bedrooms with hot and cold water; adequate bath and lavatory arrangements. Meals are provided for the residents but their availability to non-residents may be limited.

** Hotels offering a higher standard of accommodation and some private bathrooms/showers. A wider choice of food is provided but the availability of meals to non-residents may be limited.

*** Well-appointed hotels with more spacious accommodation with a large number of bedrooms with private bathrooms/showers. Fuller meal facilities are provided, but luncheon and weekend service to non-residents may be restricted.

**** Exceptionally well-appointed hotels offering a high standard of comfort and service with the majority of bedrooms providing private bathrooms/showers.

***** Luxury hotels offering the highest international standards.

(ap) Hotels which conform to most star classification requirements and are worthy of recommendation.

🌲🌳 The symbol used to denote an AA country-house hotel where a relaxed informal atmosphere and personal welcome prevail. However, some of the facilities may differ from those found in urban hotels of the same classification. These hotels are often secluded but not always rurally situated.

White stars

This method is used to indicate establishments high in amenities but with deliberately limited personalised services, designed and operated to cater predominantly for short stay guests. Under this heading will be found some motels and motor hotels, with bedroom facilities mainly on a self-service basis. It is emphasised that white stars are an indication of a type of hotel.

Red stars

The award used to denote hotels considered to be of outstanding merit within their classification.

Subjective awards

In addition to the classification granted to indicate the scope and range of services and facilities provided by appointed hotels, the AA assesses them subjectively to highlight aspects of their operation which are of particular merit. Applications for these awards are unnecessary as each hotel is automatically considered at the time of the annual inspection.

Merit symbols
H Hospitality — friendliness and quality of service
B Bedrooms
L Lounges, bars and public areas
These symbols are used to denote particular aspects of the hotel's operation which are considered significantly above the standard applied by the star classification granted, but not necessarily above that expected from a hotel in a higher classification.

AA rosette awards in hotel dining rooms and restaurants
AA rosettes were introduced to highlight hotels and restaurants where it was judged that the food could be specially recommended.
A single rosette is an indication that the food is of a higher standard than could normally be expected in a hotel or restaurant within a particular classification.
Two rosettes are awarded where the hotels are judged to offer very much above-the-average food, irrespective of classification.
Three rosettes are the supreme award for those hotels where the food is considered outstanding.

1.3 HOTEL ORGANISATION

Organisation means the arrangement of staff and the allocation of their duties and responsibilities so that the whole establishment functions as one unit. It is important that there are clear lines of authority and good lines of communication.

The organisation of a hotel will depend on its size and type. In a small hotel (Fig. 1.1) the organisation is comparatively simple, with a manager or manageress supervising all the areas of operation. Communications are therefore usually direct and easy, and the staff are able to relate their work personally to that of other departments.

As a hotel increases in size, however, the tasks have to be subdivided into separate

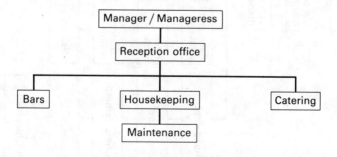

Figure 1.1 *Organisation of a small hotel*

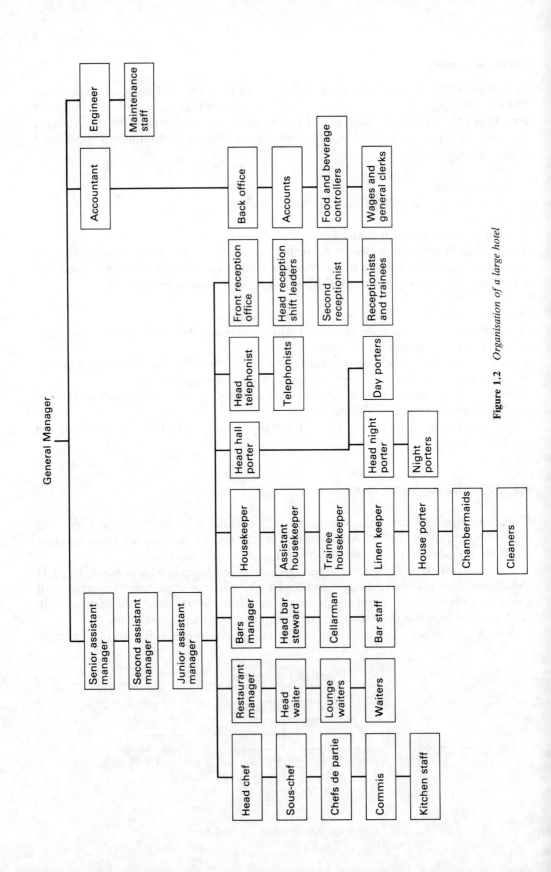

Figure 1.2 *Organisation of a large hotel*

areas of work and supervised by section heads; and in a very large hotel (Fig. 1.2) the volume of work is such that under departmental heads staff specialise in one aspect of the work only and there is little opportunity to relate their individual efforts to the whole operation.

Figures 1.3, 1.4 and 1.5, are examples of the management structure of some hotels, but it must be remembered that these diagrams are only examples and what is suitable for one type of hotel is not necessarily suitable for another.

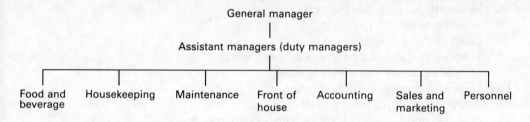

Figure 1.3 *Management structure of a large hotel*

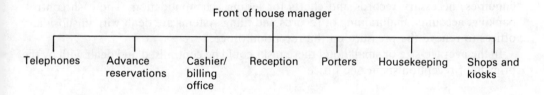

Figure 1.4 *Front office structure of a large hotel*

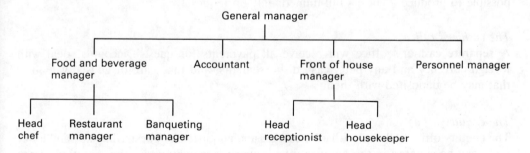

Figure 1.5 *Organisation chart for a medium-sized hotel*

The function of the reception office

In all hotels the reception office is the focal point. Receptionists are expected to be charming, tactful, diplomatic and capable of dealing with members of the public as well as carrying out the innumerable tasks that ensure the smooth and efficient running of the office.

Whether that office is a small centralised office of a medium-sized hotel, or the front office of a large hotel with clearly defined areas for advance reservations, cashier and billing, accounts, telephone and front desk reception, its function is to:

1.   Sell accommodation.
2.   Receive and welcome guests.
3.   Check-in and register guests.
4.   Check-out guests and deal with the settlement of their accounts.
5.   Handle enquiries and complaints and provide information.
6.   Deal with advance reservations.
7.   Allocate rooms.
8.   Chart all reservations.
9.   Keep up-to-the-minute records of room status.
10.   Handle incoming and outgoing mail.
11.   Deal with telephone communications.
12.   Attend to all duplicating and photocopying.
13.   Maintain good communications with all departments.

The billing office has to ensure that charges are posted correctly to the guest's folio (bill). The accounts office has to deal with all aspects of the accounts system.

In large hotels the front reception office is basically the sales department dealing with enquiries, necessary records and charts for letting accommodation. The cash control, banking, accounts, maintaining of records and filing systems are dealt with in subsidiary offices to relieve the pressure on the reception office.

In the average-size or small hotel these tasks could be centralised and dealt with by the brigade of receptionists in one office.

The billing office
This section of the front office concentrates on the recording of the daily sales and charges on the guests' bills. Billing machines and the tabular ledger are used in the preparation of accounts and the work must always be up to the minute, as it should be possible to produce a guest's bill immediately on request.

The cashier's office
A separate cashier's office will receive all payments for guests' accounts, deal with foreign currency and any petty cash disbursements, and take care of guests' valuables that may be deposited with them.

The enquiry office
The enquiry office will deal with all messages and enquiries for guests. The key and letter racks can be situated in the enquiry office, which is usually under the direction of the head porter.

The uniformed staff
The number of uniformed staff will depend on the size of the hotel. Figure 1.6 shows the uniformed staff for a large hotel.

The head porter is responsible for the supervision and allocation of duties to all the uniformed staff, works in close liaison with the reception office, and usually keeps a log book recording all the various happenings and events during the day. The head porter

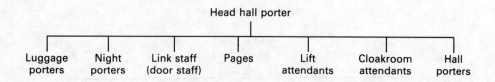

Figure 1.6

needs to have an exceptional memory for names and faces, and be a fountain of knowledge in order to deal with the numerous enquiries of the guests.

The night porters usually work eight p.m. to eight a.m. shift, performing all the duties that the day porters would be required to do. They are responsible for the security of the building during the night and will often be required to operate the telephone switchboard if there is no telephonist on duty. It is customary for the night porter to leave a report for the oncoming morning shift, detailing late arrivals and departures, special happenings or instructions regarding the guests.

The housekeeping department

Under the supervision of the head housekeeper, this department is responsible for maintaining the bedrooms and public rooms in a clean and sanitary condition. There must always be good communications and liaison between the reception office and housekeeping department, because in order to sell accommodation efficiently the receptionist must be kept informed by the housekeeping department of the exact status of all rooms at all times.

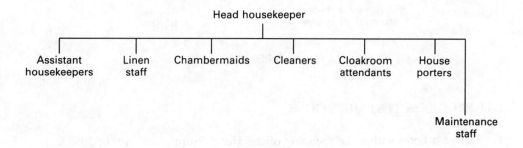

Figure 1.7

Restaurants and bars

The restaurant manager has the responsibility for the organisation and administration of the restaurants, bars and other food and beverage service areas. In a large, well-appointed hotel the service of food and drink will be organised on the lines indicated in Fig. 1.8.

Kitchens

The *chef de cuisine* (head chef) has the responsibility for the organisation and supervision of the kitchens. A large hotel or restaurant kitchen, preparing meals of the highest international standard, is traditionally organised as shown in Fig. 1.9.

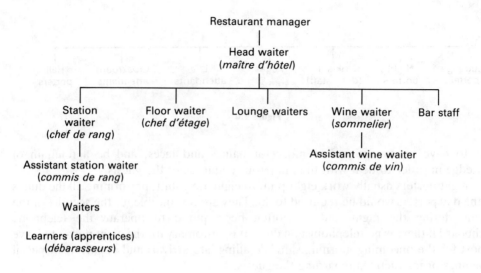

Figure 1.8

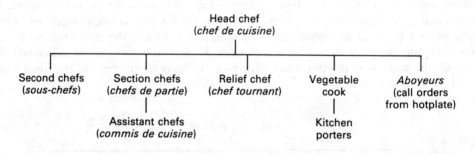

Figure 1.9

1.4 PROGRESS TEST QUESTIONS

1. Define a hotel within the meaning of the Hotel Proprietors' Act of 1956.
2. What responsibilities and liabilities are proprietors expected to assume with regard to their guests?
3. Give five different categories of hotel.
4. Explain the basic principles of good hotel organisation.
5. Describe briefly the basic function of the reception office, enumerating the services it provides.
6. Explain the following terms:
    (a) *maître d'hôtel*
    (b) *chef de cuisine*
    (c) *sous-chef*
    (d) *sommelier*
    (e) *chef de rang*
    (f) *chef de partie*
    (g) *chef d'étage*

2 [...]ls

2.1 [...] PTIONIST

The re[...] entre of the hotel. Not only is it the communication centre [...]nts, it is also the first point of contact for incoming visitors [...] the outgoing. Therefore, the receptionist, whether male or [...]ole to play in the establishment.

Many [...] first-class receptionist; some of these qualities, such as charm [...]naturally, but others can be acquired by good training and the c[...]ous development of social skills and personal attributes.

A smile of welcome from a charming, attractive, well-spoken receptionist immediately creates a warm, friendly atmosphere for the often weary traveller on arrival. But a capable, competent, intelligent person is also needed to ensure that the many tasks that have to be dealt with every day in the office are carried out smoothly and efficiently, and that good relationships and communications with all other departments in the hotel are maintained.

2.2 POISE AND DEPORTMENT

The term 'poise' is difficult to define — it is the self-discipline that enables you to appear serenely dignified when your head is throbbing, your feet aching and you are confronted with an irate guest full of complaints. Poise is the ability to be friendly yet businesslike, to suggest efficiency without frenzied effort, to be self-assured without appearing smug.

Poise is directly concerned with good deportment; a poised person does not walk noisily or clumsily, slump in a chair, or sit or bend down in an ungainly manner. You should walk with a brisk step which indicates that you are interested in your job, never slouch along, droop your shoulders or flop awkwardly in a chair; your head should be held high, your shoulders back; you should walk gracefully with good body line, and sit and bend down elegantly. Aim for neat foot and hand movements and a graceful carriage. Remember, poise and good deportment can be cultivated, and achieving them will give a sense of well-being and an improved mental attitude, for you can never feel completely at ease if you are self-conscious about your appearance and movements.

2.3 PERSONAL APPEARANCE AND HYGIENE

Anyone who has to deal with the public or who is in continual contact with other people as part of their job must always be aware that attention to their appearance and personal hygiene is of the utmost importance. It does not take much imagination to realise the bad impression that can be created by a person who has greasy unkempt hair, unclean or unpressed clothes, laddered stockings or tights, dirty down-at-the-heel shoes, chewed or dirty fingernails or unfortunately halitosis (bad breath) or body odour. It is essential that a receptionist, whether male or female, should appear on duty immaculate in every way. Therefore, a regular daily routine should be developed so that care of personal appearance and hygiene is automatic.

Hair

Extremes in hair style are not advocated whilst on duty. Neat well-groomed hair cut in a style that suits the face and personality is much more pleasing. When bending over a desk the top of the head is often presented; therefore, the hair must always be clean and free of dandruff, and not trailing over the paperwork.

Complexion and make-up

There are many aids to beauty available and no lack of advice on the correct use of make-up, but one should bear in mind that use of it should be discreet and not overdone. Good eating habits, plenty of fresh fruit and vegetables, and, of course, a reasonable amount of sleep all lend themselves to good health, which in turn will be reflected in a clear skin and bright eyes which are attractive in themselves.

Hands

Hands are always on display and nothing looks more unsightly than broken fingernails, highly coloured chipped nail varnish or chewed nails. Well manicured hands with a carefully toned nail varnish are much more attractive.

Clothing

Many hotels provide uniforms for their staff to be worn when on duty. Uniforms should be kept fresh and crisp. If one is permitted to wear clothes of one's own choice, they should be smart and attractive, but extremes in fashion should be avoided and colour kept discreet. A spare pair of stockings or tights should always be handy as nothing looks so unattractive as laddered tights. Shoes should be smart but comfortable, for receptionists may have to spend many hours on their feet.

Halitosis

Halitosis (bad breath) can be very unpleasant. The causes of it are numerous. Sensible diet and regular brushing of teeth will obviously help, but one should visit the dentist at least once every six months for a check up. If the problem of halitosis persists, a visit to the doctor is necessary to determine the cause.

Body odour

Like halitosis, body odour can be extremely unpleasant and embarrassing. Regular bathing and daily use of an anti-perspirant or a good deodorant will normally ensure personal freshness, but if the problem persists, a visit to the doctor is necessary.

2.4 THE VOICE AND SPEECH

The receptionist is in constant oral communication with the public; therefore, the voice must be pleasing and manner of speech correct. Clear enunciation of sounds is very important, particularly when speaking into the telephone. Slovenly speech is a bad habit, for example, saying 'aving' instead of 'having', 'jer know' instead of 'do you know', 'jist' instead of 'just', and using slang such as 'OK, Yeh, ain't it, arf a mo, hang on'. If it is possible, listen to a tape recording of your voice, note the defects and consciously practise clear enunciation and correct pronunciation.

2.5 TELEPHONE MANNER

A good receptionist must develop a telephone personality — remembering that you cannot be seen, only heard. The voice must be well modulated, the spoken words clear and distinct, and the tone of voice must be friendly, interested and helpful. It should never sound mechanical, indifferent or impatient.

The following simple rules will help develop a good telephone manner and technique:

1. Answer the telephone promptly and make a habit of picking up a pencil and notepad at the same time — being kept waiting will make the caller impatient.
2. Greet the caller pleasantly with: 'good morning', 'good afternoon' or 'good evening' — never 'hallo' — and then identify the establishment, e.g. 'Imperial Hotel', or if an internal call, answer: 'good morning, reception desk'.
3. Callers usually respond by giving their name and stating their business, but if they do not, tactfully ask: 'who is calling please?' or 'may I help you?'.
4. Listen attentively, and if information or details have to be recorded, write them down clearly and legibly, as they are given.
5. If a message has to be taken, be certain to record the date, time of message, who it is for, and who it is from, and always repeat the message back to the caller to ensure that the details are correct.
6. When receiving incoming calls for executives or management, always ascertain who the caller is and, if possible, the nature of his or her business, and then check whether the member of staff wishes to accept the call. Busy executives should not be bothered by trifling matters, so the receptionist must learn how to classify calls and route them to the person best suited to deal with them.

Example 1
Receptionist: Good morning, Imperial Hotel.
Caller: May I speak to the manager?
Receptionist: Who is calling, please?
Caller: Mrs Jones. I have a room booked for the thirtieth of July and I'd like a word with the manager.
Receptionist: *(Quickly checking the advance booking chart)* Oh! Yes, Mrs Jones, we have a room booked for you on the thirtieth of July — can I be of any assistance to you?
Caller: Well, I just wanted to ask the manager if it is all right to bring my poodle with me? She does fret if I leave her behind.
Receptionist: That will be quite all right, Mrs Jones. The hotel has facilities for small

dogs at a charge of 90p per day, but I am afraid they are not allowed in the public rooms.

Caller: Oh, that's fine.
Receptionist: Would you like me to make arrangements for your poodle, Mrs Jones?
Caller: Yes, please. Thank you very much.

In this telephone conversation the receptionist tactfully ascertained the nature of the call, realised that it could be dealt with without bothering a busy manager, dealt with the matter according to established policy and reassured the caller.

Example 2
Receptionist: Good afternoon, Imperial Hotel.
Caller: This is the secretary of the Sidham Sailing Club. I'm phoning about our dinner on the twelfth of November; I want to discuss the seating arrangements.
Receptionist: Just one moment, please. You will want to talk to our Mr Wyatt, the assistant manager and function controller, who deals with all our function bookings. May I have your name, please?
Caller: Mr Williams.
Receptionist: If you will please hold the line a moment I will see if Mr Wyatt is available. *(The receptionist then locates Mr Wyatt as quickly as possible and informs him that there is a call from Mr Williams, Secretary of the Sailing Club, who wishes to discuss the seating arrangements for their dinner on the twelfth of November. This will alert Mr Wyatt to the nature of the call. The call is then put through.)*

2.6 TACT AND DIPLOMACY

Diplomacy is the art of conducting negotiations between people.

Tact is the skill of handling a difficult person or situation without giving offence.

The day-to-day experience of dealing with people and problems will develop the skills of tact and diplomacy. It is not difficult to deal with people who are pleasant and co-operative, but it requires intelligence, understanding, common sense and self-discipline to handle difficult and awkward people or situations without giving offence and putting yourself or the management in the wrong.

The following examples illustrate the type of situation that could call for the utmost in tact and diplomacy.

Example 1
Guests in the restaurant have reason to complain about their dinner. They have already complained to the waiter without satisfaction, so they have descended on the reception desk demanding to see the manager. The manager is not available and the receptionist on duty has to handle the matter.

In this position it is absolutely essential that the receptionist remains cool, calm and in control of the situation. The exact cause of the complaint has to be ascertained. The kitchen and restaurant staff must be contacted immediately and the cause for complaint dealt with. The guests must be persuaded to return to the restaurant, where it is imperative they be served with a more than satisfactory meal and be completely pacified.

As you can imagine, the receptionist in this situation will require patience, self-control, initiative, resourcefulness, understanding and persuasiveness. Needless to say, the receptionist will have to be the soul of tact and diplomacy.

Example 2

A guest, Mr Green, is dining in the restaurant with a young lady, when another lady purporting to be his wife arrives at the reception desk and asks that her husband be paged.

To avoid any possible embarrassment the receptionist should show the lady to a seat in the lounge. She should then telephone through to the restaurant manager who will be asked to see that Mr Green is discreetly informed that his wife wishes to speak to him at the reception desk. If the public address system has to be used for paging Mr Green, the words for the announcement should be very carefully chosen, for example: 'Will Mr Green please come to the reception desk'.

Example 3

An urgent message is received for a guest, Mrs Jones. The caller asks if she can be informed as gently as possible that a very close relative has died. The hotel manager is at a very important meeting and the receptionist is asked if she could cope and deal with the difficult task of breaking the news to Mrs Jones. This is a problem which again requires the utmost tact and diplomacy, for one can never be sure of the reaction of a guest on hearing sad news.

In a situation like this, it would be advisable to use the privacy of the manager's office, order a pot of tea or coffee and have a drink of brandy or something similar handy. Then send a message to the guest, Mrs Jones, making sure it does not alarm her, asking her if she could possibly call at the manager's office. On her arrival, you invite her to sit down and offer her a cup of tea or coffee, which will have a calming effect, and then, as gently as possible, you break the news, and offer every possible assistance for any arrangements she may have to make.

When dealing with any manner of complaint by a guest:

1. The name and room number of the person making the complaint should be noted.
2. The exact nature of the complaint should be ascertained.
3. The guest must be assured that the complaint, no matter how trivial, will be dealt with immediately.
4. The complaint should be investigated by contacting the departmental supervisor of the area concerned.

Example 4

A guest complains to the reception office that she has no soap in her bathroom and the towels had not been changed. The receptionist will ascertain the name and the room number of the guest, apologise to the guest for the oversight and reassure her that the matter will be dealt with immediately. The reception office will then contact the housekeeping department, informing them of the complaint, who should then deal with the matter immediately.

2.7 DEALING WITH VERBAL ENQUIRIES

All verbal enquiries should be dealt with quickly and efficiently. The receptionist should learn how to extract from the caller the exact nature of the information required in order to classify the enquiry. The reception office should be so organised that all sources of information necessary to answer enquiries are immediately to hand. The layout of the hotel, the organisation and the names of all persons responsible for the function of servicing departments should be learnt thoroughly so the calls can be routed to the persons best suited to deal with them.

2.8   ENQUIRIES THAT ARE USUALLY DEALT WITH BY THE RECEPTION DESK

Reservations
To deal with enquiries referring to reservations the receptionist must have to hand the up-to-the-minute room availability chart; the advance booking chart; the bookings diary; and the hotel tariff. (These will be dealt with in detail in Chapter 3.) By referring to these the receptionist will be able to inform the enquirer as to the availability of accommodation and give details of the charges and facilities of the hotel.

Information for guests
It is sometimes quite incredible the kind of information people expect the reception desk to supply, but generally it takes the form of questions about train, bus and taxi services, which means up-to-date timetables and the telephone numbers of the local taxi services must be to hand. Enquiries regarding the geographical location and other details of places of interest require the receptionist to know the locality well and have a guide book on the area. Details of activities and entertainments going on in the town can be obtained from the entertainments page in the local press. The local guide book will provide information on local churches and public services. The *Post Office Guide* will give details of the postal services, and of course the receptionist will be expected to know the local hairdressers, doctors, dentists, shops, restaurants, bars and clubs.

Foreign visitors will expect the receptionist to have a very good knowledge of the country in general. So guide books on London, the stately homes of England, places of historical interest and beauty spots in Great Britain should be studied.

Information regarding guests
The guest is entitled to a measure of privacy and protection and any enquiries asking for information about guests should be handled with caution and the utmost discretion. One must avoid publicity or anything that could damage the reputation of the hotel. The Police, Home Office officials, and people holding a court warrant are the only persons who may inspect the hotel register on demand, but then only in the presence of the management in the privacy of an office. Anyone else asking for information should immediately be referred to the manager who will take the responsibility of dealing with the enquiry.

2.9   COMMUNICATION WITH THE GUESTS

Every employee is the personal representative of the establishment and has a public relations job to do. To establish good communication with the guests is part of this job; they are paying for service and how much nicer that service is if it is given with a smile by a person who takes a personal interest! There should always be a willingness to help and an understanding of the guests' anxieties and problems.

Always greet the guest warmly by name and say something pleasant, never argue or contradict, and avoid controversial conversation. Do not be too familiar, and remember that 'Sir' or 'Madam' is not a sign of servility but one of respect. Immediate attention to requests for information is part of the service that the guest will appreciate. It is not difficult to please nine out of ten people, so regard the difficult and awkward customer as a challenge which will prove your skill in human relations.

2.10 PROGRESS TEST QUESTIONS

1. Write a short paragraph on the desirable qualities of a good receptionist.
2. Write briefly how you, as a receptionist, would deal with the situation where guests complain that their room has not been cleaned and they have had to wait over a half an hour for room service.
3. 'Attention to personal appearance and hygiene are of the utmost importance to a receptionist.' Discuss this statement.
4. What are the essentials of a good telephone voice?
5. Explain how you would deal with an agitated lady on the telephone who wants to speak to the manager because she thinks she left her watch on the washbasin of her room when she checked out.
6. The secretary of the local tennis club telephones to say that he wants to make a booking for their annual dinner and dance. Detail what action you would take.
7. You receive a telephone call from the husband of a guest who happens to be out for a stroll. He asks if you would inform her as soon as possible that her son has had a serious accident and would she go straight to the hospital. Describe how you would deal with the situation.
8. A guest, Mr Prentice, is attending an important luncheon being held at the hotel; a very hysterical lady who says she is Mrs Prentice comes to the reception desk and demands that Mr Prentice be found as she wishes to speak to him. Explain what action you would take to avoid embarrassment to Mr Prentice and the hotel.

3 Reception

Irrespective of whether a hotel is small, medium or large the basic work of the reception office is the same, selling accommodation, receiving and welcoming guests, maintaining accounting and other records, liaison with all other departments within the hotel and integrating all activities relating to the service and comfort of the guests.

Whether the reception office has all the latest computerised equipment or whether aids and records are manually operated, good hotel reception is based on procedures and principles applicable to all types of hotel and the following tasks have to be dealt with:

(a) reservations;
(b) room allocation;
(c) registering of guests;
(d) guest accounting;
(e) departure of guests;
(f) guest history records;
(g) management information;
(h) control procedures of the front office;
(i) reports and statistics.

These tasks will be dealt with in detail in the following chapters.

Large hotels never close, and operate a 24-hour service, 365 days a year. The reception desk is usually staffed by a brigade of receptionists working a rota system of 3 shifts to ensure a 24-hour coverage; for example, 8 a.m. to 3 p.m., 3 p.m. to 11 p.m. and 11 p.m. to 8 a.m. On the late shift the desk and telephone switchboard are often covered by a skeleton staff or a night porter.

Most hotels have periods of high activity and low activity and therefore it is quite common practice to organise the duty rotas for certain members of staff on a 'split duty' basis. This simply means that the normal 8-hour duty shift is split; for example, 4 hours on duty, 2 hours off duty, then 4 hours on duty, or 4 hours in the morning and 4 hours in the evening, or whatever combination lends itself to the efficient running of the hotel.

The busiest time and peak hours of the reception office will depend on the type of hotel. At hotels near airports and in major cities visitors are arriving and departing at all times with peak periods being the morning departures and arrivals building up during late afternoon and early evening. In residential or seasonal holiday resorts where guests stay for a week or more the busiest time for the reception office is usually Friday, Saturday or Sunday with the peak period for arrivals and departures being Saturday. The head receptionist is usually responsible for planning the rotas to ensure that the reception desk is adequately staffed for peak periods and throughout the week. For the hotel and catering industry split duties, weekends, Christmas, Easter and bank holidays are normal working periods. However, most people who join the industry feel that the interesting nature of the work and career opportunities more than compensate for the unusual hours they are expected to work.

Layout of reception area (Fig. 3.1)

The design, colours used and decor of the reception area will depend entirely on the tastes and policies of each individual hotel or group of hotels. The first impression the guest will have on arrival will be the front desk, so obviously the counter and receptionists must be pleasing to the eye. However, the reception office is very much a functional working area and should be well planned with work centres focused around the major equipment used, and located so that communication and liaison with the other sections is easy, simple and efficient.

3.1 THE RECEPTION AREA

It is the responsibility of the staff to see that the reception area is immaculate at all times and when arriving on duty the shift should check the following:

1. The reception counter should be free from dust and any display literature should be up to date, neat and tidy and in its correct place.
2. Ashtrays should be emptied and cleaned throughout the day.
3. Flower arrangements must have fresh water and dead flowers and leaves must be removed. If artificial flowers are used they must be dusted.

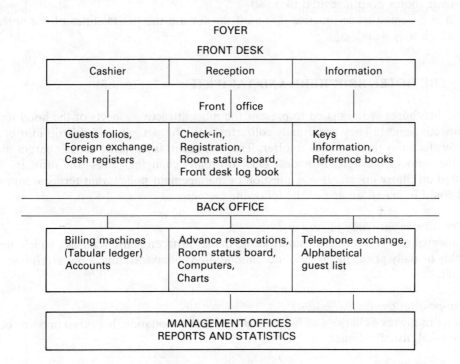

Figure 3.1 *Simple layout of reception area*

4. A clean sheet of blotting paper should be in the blotter.
5. A good usable pen or biro should be available in or attached to a stand.
6. Desk calendars should always show the correct date.
7. The Tourism (Sleeping Accommodation Price Display) Order 1977, which became effective in 1978, requires that the the tariff showing rates for each type of room to be displayed at the reception desk in a prominent position (see Chapter 8). The Hotel Proprietors Act of 1956 is similarly displayed in a prominent position.

There are certain basic rules of behaviour which the management expect their reception staff to follow:

1. It is unfair to other members of staff to be late on duty as they cannot leave a reception desk unattended.
2. Reception staff should neither smoke or eat food in the reception area.
3. It is considered bad manners for reception staff to address a visitor from a sitting position; they should always rise and be attentive when someone approaches the counter.
4. It is ungainly and slovenly to lean or lounge on a counter or desk.
5. It is ill mannered to stand around gossiping, as nothing is more irritating to a person waiting for attention.
6. Always be prepared to listen patiently to a guest's chatter no matter how boring, but develop a technique of being able to detach, oneself politely from a conversation without giving offence, especially if there is work to be done or other people waiting for attention.
7. The management usually have a ruling that receptionists do not socialise with the guests on a personal basis; therefore staff should not make dates with guests or visit their rooms even if invited to do so.
8. It is accepted trade practice that staff do not use the bar facilities of the hotel at which they work.

3.2 THE HOTEL BROCHURE AND TARIFF (Fig. 3.2, Fig. 3.3)

Hotel brochures are designed to present the most attractive aspects of the hotel to the prospective guest. They are usually colourful with photographs and descriptions of the various facilities the hotel has to offer. The hotel tariff is the structure of charges made for the services the hotel provides. Due to rapidly changing prices, the tariff is often printed on flimsy inserts. It is a question of management policy what terms are quoted and could be based on any of the following systems:

En pension terms (fully inclusive)
Residential and resort hotels usually quote in the tariff 'en pension terms', which means weekly or daily prices inclusive of accommodation, breakfast, luncheon, afternoon tea, dinner.

Demi-pension terms (half-board)
The terms means a charge which is inclusive of accommodation, breakfast and one other main meal, usually dinner.

AA   **THE GRAND HOTEL**   RAC
WESTBOURNE

****

Telephone
Westbourne (0323) 12345   Telex 66660

TARIFF

(Excluding Christmas, Easter and bank holidays)
Rates are per person per room and
inclusive of service charge and VAT at 15%.
All rooms have private bathroom, radio and colour TV.

	Apartment with Breakfast		Full Pension	
	Daily	Weekly rate	Daily	Weekly rate
	£	£	£	£
Inland room	17.00	114.00	25.00	170.00
Sea view room	19.00	129.00	27.00	184.00
Single room	Supplementary charge of £2.00 per day			
Suites	Tariff on application			

Apartment and breakfast includes early morning tea and full English breakfast.
Full pension (minimum 3 days) includes early morning tea, English breakfast, 4 course luncheon,
afternoon tea, dinner with coffee.
Children (sharing parents room): no charge.
Children under 14 (separate room: 75% of normal tariff.
Children under 14 (sharing room): 50% of normal tariff.
Dogs welcome except in restaurant and lounges: £2.00 per day.

Meal prices (inclusive of service charge and VAT 15%)

Luncheon with coffee	£5.50
Afternoon tea	£1.75
Dinner with coffee	£7.50

Weekend breaks:
Conferences, private functions: terms quoted on request.

Prices are subject to change without notice.

Figure 3.2 *Typical tariff of a resort hotel*

Bed and breakfast terms

Some tariffs quote terms which include the accommodation and breakfast. Breakfast can be 'continental', which consists of croissants (rolls) and butter with jam and either coffee or tea. A full 'English' breakfast would include fruit juice, cereal, sometimes kippers or smoked haddock, bacon or sausages, eggs, tomatoes, toast, marmalade, and tea or coffee, usually at an extra charge.

TARIFF

THE
ROYAL HOTEL
LONDON
★★★★

Telephone   Telex 33315
01 · 342 · 4561   Direct reservations: 01 · 243 · 1654

Bedrooms

Single room with private bath   £40.00 per night

Twin/double room with private bath   £54.00 per night

Triple room with private bath   £74.00 per night

All rooms have private bath and shower, colour TV and radio, direct-dial telephone, electric
trouser press and private bar.

All room rates include service charge
and VAT at 15%

Suites

Single room with sitting room   £95.00 per night

Twin/double room with sitting room   £108.00 per night

Suite rates include service charge and VAT at 15%

Breakfast

English breakfast   £5.00
Continental breakfast   £3.00

* Children under 5 accommodated free.
* Children over 5 and under 14 accommodated in room with an adult are charged at a £1.00 per
  night per child.
* Children under 14 accommodated in their own bedroom are charged 75% of the normal tariff.

Prices are subject to change without notice.

Conferences, exhibitions, receptions, banquets, meetings.

TARIFF ON REQUEST

Figure 3.3 *Typical tariff of a large transient hotel*

Separate charges
Many large hotels quote separate charges for their services. The accommodation price is quoted either as a price for the room, or a price per person per room, with meals charged to the guest's account as they are taken.

Other terminology

Rack rate — This term is used to describe the full tariff rate for accommodation.
R & B — Room and breakfast.
Discounted rate — A percentage is deducted from the rack rate.
Special rate — Hotels often quote a special rate for functions, groups, tours, businessmen or certain organisations who use the hotel on a regular basis.
Continental plan — Room and breakfast.
American plan — This term is used to describe full board terms to include accommodation, breakfast, luncheon, afternoon tea and dinner.
Inclusive terms — The same as American plan.
Modified American plan — Room, breakfast and one main meal.
European plan — This term is used to describe the charge for accommodation only.
Half-board — Accommodation, breakfast and one main meal, either luncheon or dinner.
Low season — The time of year when business is at its quietest, usually the winter months when the lowest tariff prices are quoted.
High or peak season — The time of year, usually the holiday and summer periods, when the highest tariff prices are quoted.
Shoulder period — The mid-seasons, usually spring and autumn when a mid-tariff price is quoted.

3.3 THE ADVANCE RESERVATION OFFICE

The staff who work in the reservation section have a great deal of responsibility and it is their task to see that all reservations are dealt with promptly and efficiently. Rooms must be allocated and charted on the reservation and room status charts so that not only the clients get the type of accommodation they have requested but also the hotel achieves the maximum occupancy of the rooms.

The first indication that a person requires accommodation is through a request for a reservation. This can be by letter, telex, telephone, through a central reservation service, or as a walk-in or chance guest at the desk.

Whenever a request for accommodation is received the receptionist must establish:

(a) the guest's name;
(b) the arrival date;
(c) the length of stay;
(d) the departure date;
(e) the type of room required.

With this information the receptionist is able to check the availability of accommodation.

```
┌─────────────────────────────────────────────────────────────────────────────┐
│              * * * *   GRAND HOTEL   * * * *                                   │
│                 Westbourne, Sussex                                            │
│                  Tel. 0323 – 12345                                            │
│                     RESERVATION                                               │
├───────────────────────────────────────┬───────────────────────────────────────┤
│ Name                                   │ Date                                  │
│                                        ├──────────────────────────────┬────────┤
│ Address                                │ Date of arrival              │        │
│                                        │ Time of arrival              │        │
│ Telephone No.                          │ Date of departure            │        │
│                                        │ Time of departure            │        │
│ NATIONALITY                            │ Number of guests             │        │
├───────────────────────────────────────┴──────────────────────────────┴────────┤
│        TYPE OF ACCOMMODATION              METHOD OF PAYMENT                     │
│                                           (Please tick)                        │
│           ☐ Single/B                        ☐ Cash                             │
│           ☐ Twin/B                          ☐ Cheque                           │
│           ☐ Double/B                        ☐ Credit card                      │
│           ☐ Suite                                                              │
├────────────────────────────────────────────────────────────────────────────────┤
│ SPECIAL INSTRUCTIONS:                                                          │
│                                                                                │
├────────────────────────────────────────────────────────────────────────────────┤
│ FOR HOTEL USE ONLY                                                             │
│ Room allocated ...........................   Number of guests .................│
│ Key No. ..................................   Children..........................│
│ Rate code ................................   Deposit in advance................│
│ Reservation clerk's signature .................................................│
└────────────────────────────────────────────────────────────────────────────────┘
```

Figure 3.4 *Reservation form*

The reservation form (Fig. 3.4)

People requiring accommodation often make use of the reservation form which hotels include in their hotel brochure. The reservation forms are specifically designed to provide all the necessary details and information required to process the booking, that is:

(a) date of receipt of reservation;
(b) name, address and nationality of the client;
(c) date and time of expected arrival;
(d) length of stay;
(e) date of departure;
(f) method of payment, e.g. cash, cheque, credit card;
(g) advance deposit;
(h) any special requirement, e.g. garage, special diet, requirements for children or pets;
(i) signature of clerk processing reservation.

The Grange
Mews Avenue
London S.W.1.

7th March 1984

The Manager
The Grand Hotel
Westbourne
Sussex

Dear Sir,

We would like to book a twin-bedded room with bath and a single room with bath for one week from 1st May 1984.

We would if possible like to be on the 5th Floor, and we would like a good view of the sea.

Thanking you in anticipation

Yours faithfully

R.L.Essex.

(R.L.ESSEX)

Figure 3.5 *Letter of enquiry*

AA   **THE GRAND HOTEL**   RAC
                           WESTBOURNE
                              * * * *

Telephone   Telex 66660
Westbourne (0323) 12345

JC/SF/M.6.

R. L. Essex Esq.,
The Grange,
Mews Avenue,
LONDON S.W.1.   10th March 19—

Dear Mr Essex

Thank you for your letter of the 7th instant requesting accommodation for
one week from 1st May 19—.

We regret we are unable to offer you rooms on the 5th floor on that date.
However, we can offer you a twin-bedded room with bathroom and a
single room with bathroom on the 4th floor which have equally splendid
views of the sea. The room appointments are identical to those on the 5th
floor.

Will you please confirm that our alternative offer is acceptable to you by
completing the enclosed Reservation Form. Also enclosed for your
information is our Brochure and Tariff.

Assuring you of our best attention.

Yours sincerely,

J. Charles

Manager
Enc

Figure 3.6   *Letter of acknowledgement*

Procedures following a request for accommodation

Enquiry by letter
1. A letter of enquiry is received (see Fig. 3.5).
2. A letter of acknowledgement (see Fig. 3.6) is sent back immediately enclosing a hotel brochure with reservation form (see Fig. 3.4) and hotel tariff (see Fig. 3.3).
3. On receipt of the reservation form, a room is allocated, and pencilled in on the advance reservation chart (see Fig. 3.10) and density chart (see Fig. 3.12) and a confirmation slip (see Fig. 3.8) is sent to the client.
4. Details from the completed reservation form are entered in the hotel's diary (see Fig. 3.9).
5. The reservation form and confirmation slip copy are then filed alphabetically in date of arrival order.
6. On the date of arrival the guest's name is typed on a card strip and inserted into the reception board (see Fig. 3.18) in the room number allocated. Coloured strips are often used to indicate VIP's or groups, and in some cases colours are used to indicate the standard of the rooms and rates, e.g. standard rate of discounted rates.
7. A name strip with the room number allocated is also typed for insertion into the alphabetical guest list, which is usually located on a rotary stand in telephone exchange area.
8. On arrival the guest must complete a registration form (see Fig. 3.8b) or sign the hotel register (see Fig. 3.21).
9. Details of the booking are entered on the room history card (see Fig. 3.33).
10. If this is the first time the guest has used the hotel a guest history card is sometimes created (see Fig. 3.35).
11. The day prior to arrival the guests' names and rooms allocated will be entered on the arrivals and departures list (see Fig. 3.27) and circulated to all heads of departments, e.g. housekeeping, restaurants, bars and accounts.
12. If a manual tabular ledger is maintained (see Chapter 5) the names of the guest will be entered on it and the guest's folio (bill) will be started.

These procedures are discussed later in the chapter. It must be remembered that not all of these records are kept by all hotels.

Confirmation slips (Fig. 3.7)

A telephone or telex request for accommodation is usually acknowledged by a 'confirmation slip' if there is time before the arrival of the guest. The confirmation slip has several copies. The top copy is sent to the client; other copies are used in the reservation office, for the allocating of rooms, charting the reservation, compiling the arrivals and departures lists and alphabetical guest list and providing information for other departments. The copies are then filed in date of arrival order.

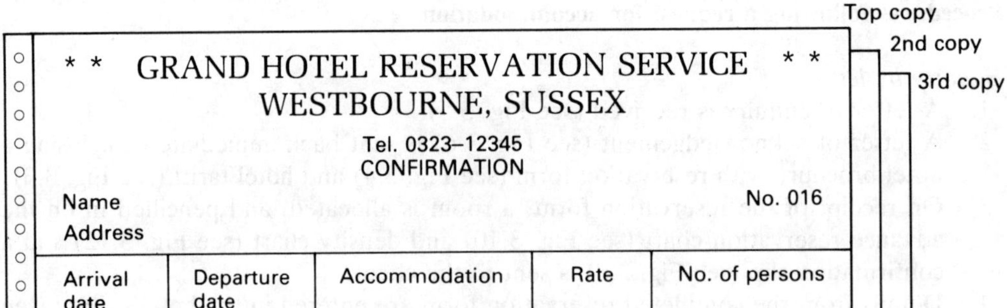

Top copy
2nd copy
3rd copy

```
* *   GRAND HOTEL RESERVATION SERVICE   * *
                WESTBOURNE, SUSSEX
                    Tel. 0323–12345
                     CONFIRMATION
Name                                                    No. 016
Address
```

Arrival date	Departure date	Accommodation	Rate	No. of persons

Arrival time	Special instructions		Meals	Special instructions

Remarks	METHOD OF PAYMENT
	Cash ☐
	Cheque in advance ☐
	Credit card ☐

Booking clerk

Please see overleaf for important information.

Figure 3.7(a)   *Confirmation slip*

ARRIVAL TIMES

* Room reservations are held until 6.00 p.m. local hotel time unless a later time is confirmed, in which case they are held until the hour specified.
* Rooms may not be available until check-out time at the hotel.
* Occupancy prior to check-out time cannot be confirmed unless payment for the previous night is authorised and guaranteed.

    EAP (early as possible) occupancy will be granted if rooms are available upon arrival at the hotel.

CANCELLATIONS/REVISIONS

* Cancellations and/or revisions of reservations must reach the destination hotel *prior* to the time specified on the reservation.
* Cancellation of a guaranteed reservation for which payment was authorised for the first night must reach destination hotel by 6.00 p.m. on the arrival date to avoid billing.
* Cancellation of a reservation for which a deposit has been sent must reach the hotel by the *date* specified on the reverse side for deposit refund or the deposit will be forfeited.
* Cancellation numbers are given at the time of cancellation and should be retained for your records.
* Revisions to arrival dates, accommodation and departure date cannot be confirmed unless accommodation is available.

RATES

* Rates are quoted in British currency.
* British currency rates are subject to fluctuations between currency exchange rate at the time of confirmation and the time of check-out.
* Applicable VAT (Value Added Tax) will be added to the hotel bill.

DEPOSIT/CANCELLATION REQUIREMENTS

* Any required deposit specified on the reverse side of the confirmation slip must reach the destination hotel by the date shown or the reservation will be cancelled.
* The deposit must be made payable to the hotel and sent to the attention of the 'front office manager'.
* A new deposit is required for revisions received after the cancellation refund deadline date.

THIS CONFIRMATION SHOULD BE PRESENTED AT THE FRONT DESK, UPON CHECK-IN. RESERVATIONS ARE *NOT* TRANSFERABLE.

Figure 3.7(b) *Reverse side of confirmation slip*

Combination confirmation slip, guest registration slip, guest folio (Fig. 3.8)

Many hotels use specially designed sets of documents to provide them with their required information. By use of NCR (no carbon required) paper whatever is typed on the top copy will be recorded on all copies, thus eliminating errors by transferring information. This method is also time- and labour-saving. The following set of documents illustrates a typical set:

(a)   the confirmation slip — with copies for records;
(b)   the guest registration slip — with copies for records;
(c)   the guest folio (bill) — with copies (see Fig. 3.8).

Perforated

File copies

***   GRAND HOTEL   ***
WESTBOURNE, SUSSEX
Tel. 0323–12345
CONFIRMATION

			Accommodation	Guaranteed arrival
Surname	Initials	Status		☐ Yes ☐ 6 p.m.

SPECIAL INSTRUCTIONS

Code rate	Arrival date	Departure date	made on	Registered	Clerk No.		
						Room No.	Folio. A15150

The Grand Hotel is pleased to confirm your requested reservation.
Please verify the accuracy of the above information.
Your reservation will be held until 6 p.m. of the indicated arrival date, unless otherwise guaranteed.
Check-out time is twelve noon. If possible a later check out will be granted with an additional charge. Please contact desk.
Check-in time is 3 p.m. Guests will be accommodated earlier whenever space is available.
Notification is required 48 hours in advance to return deposit or cancel guaranteed billing.
We look forward to the pleasure of serving you.

Sincerely
Reservations office.

FOR HOTEL USE ONLY: FIRM:

GUARANTEED BY ☐   ATTENTION OF:

TRAVEL AGENT ☐   ADDRESS:

AUTHORISED BY:

Figure 3.8(a)   *Combination confirmation slip, guest registration slip and guest folio*

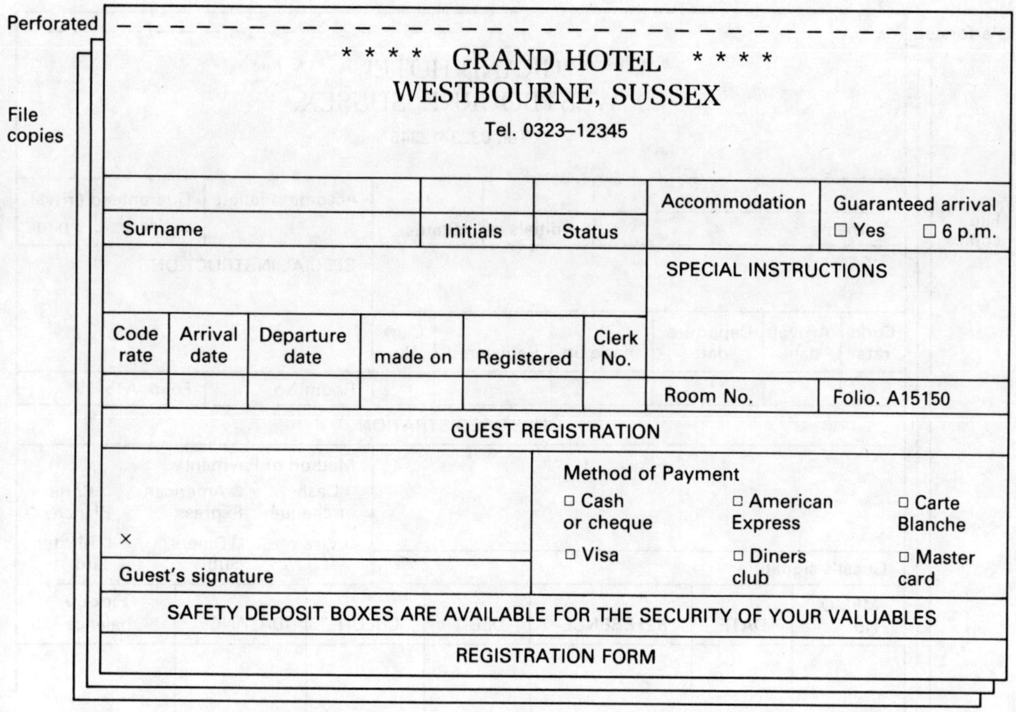

Perforated

File
copies

* * * *   **GRAND HOTEL**   * * * *
WESTBOURNE, SUSSEX
Tel. 0323–12345

							Accommodation	Guaranteed arrival
Surname			Initials	Status				☐ Yes ☐ 6 p.m.

						SPECIAL INSTRUCTIONS	

Code rate	Arrival date	Departure date	made on	Registered	Clerk No.		
						Room No.	Folio. A15150

GUEST REGISTRATION

	Method of Payment
✕	☐ Cash ☐ American ☐ Carte or cheque Express Blanche
Guest's signature	☐ Visa ☐ Diners ☐ Master club card

SAFETY DEPOSIT BOXES ARE AVAILABLE FOR THE SECURITY OF YOUR VALUABLES

REGISTRATION FORM

Figure 3.8(b)   *Guest registration*

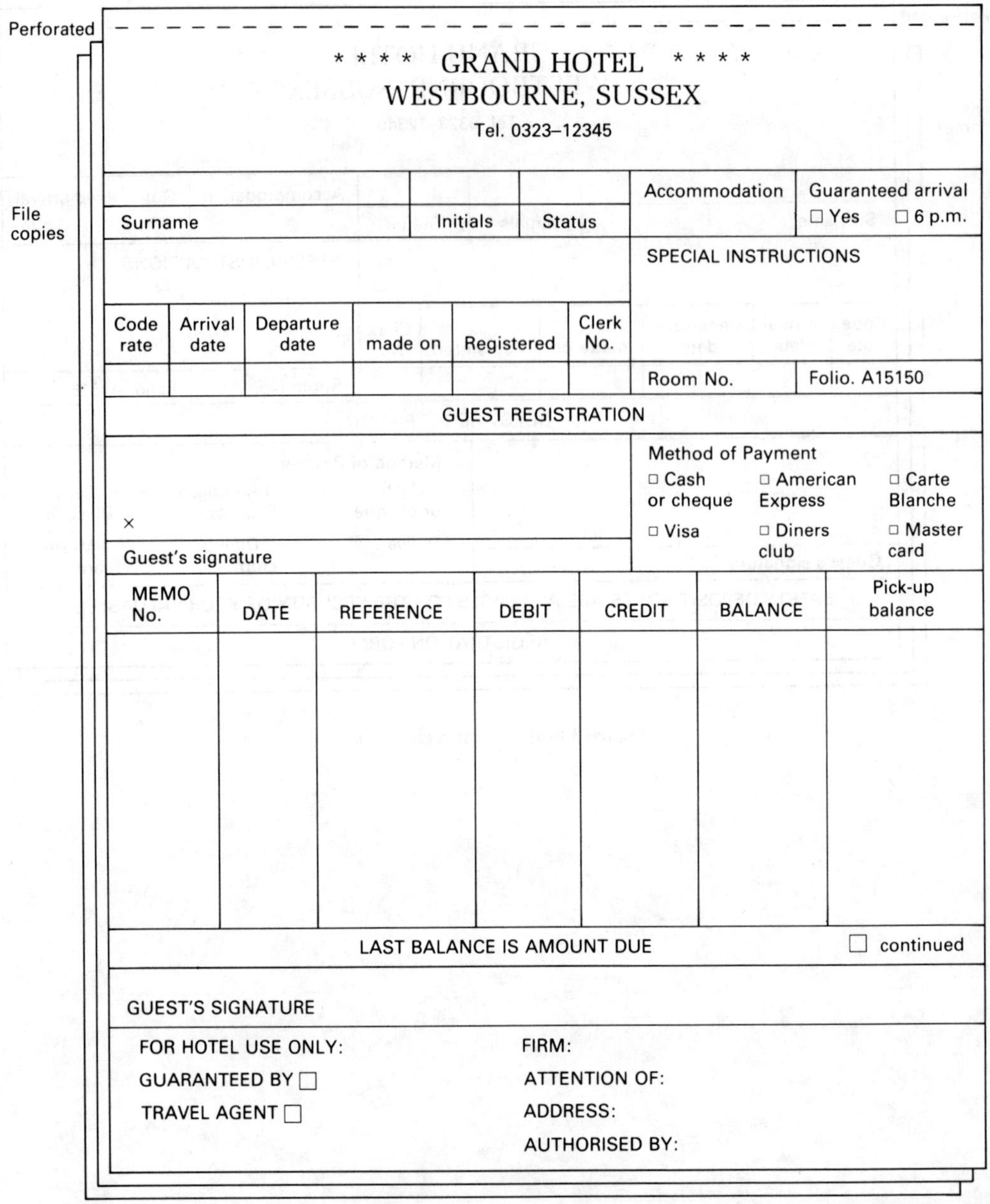

Perforated

File
copies

* * * * GRAND HOTEL * * * *
WESTBOURNE, SUSSEX
Tel. 0323–12345

Surname			Initials	Status	Accommodation	Guaranteed arrival
						☐ Yes ☐ 6 p.m.

SPECIAL INSTRUCTIONS

Code rate	Arrival date	Departure date	made on	Registered	Clerk No.	
						Room No. Folio. A15150

GUEST REGISTRATION

Method of Payment

☐ Cash or cheque   ☐ American Express   ☐ Carte Blanche

☐ Visa   ☐ Diners club   ☐ Master card

×

Guest's signature

MEMO No.	DATE	REFERENCE	DEBIT	CREDIT	BALANCE	Pick-up balance

LAST BALANCE IS AMOUNT DUE   ☐ continued

GUEST'S SIGNATURE

FOR HOTEL USE ONLY: FIRM:

GUARANTEED BY ☐   ATTENTION OF:

TRAVEL AGENT ☐   ADDRESS:

AUTHORISED BY:

Figure 3.8(c)   *Guest folio*

The hotel bookings diary (Fig. 3.9)

Some hotels maintain a hotel bookings diary, usually a large loose-leaf ledger to which pages are easily added when necessary. A separate page is used for each day, the date being clearly marked at the top of the page. When a reservation form is received or a booking confirmed the names of guests, time of arrival, length of stay and any special requirements are entered on the date of arrival page. Notes are made on VIP guests, any tour groups, seminars or special events, and the diary is used to alert and remind the front office staff of the expected activity on that day.

Room allocation

The allocation of rooms so that the hotel achieves the maximum occupancy is a task that requires skill and experience. Large hotels often have agreements with airlines or travel agents whereby they reserve a certain number of rooms each night on a guaranteed basis. These rooms are marked in on the visual advanced reservation chart automatically, as are confirmed package tours, groups, conferences and seminars. Confirmed individual reservations, walk-ins or chance guests are plotted on the chart as they occur. Colours are often used to indicate the type of booking. For example:

Red — rooms that have not been confirmed or guaranteed.
Green — rooms which have been confirmed, a deposit paid or a guarantee received.
Yellow — airline or travel agents guaranteed bookings.
Blue — groups, seminars, conferences confirmed.
Black — rooms OOO (out of order).

Unconfirmed reservations marked red on the chart usually have a three-week time limit hold period. The reservations manager will either write or telephone near that date to verify the reservation, as a 'no show' means a loss of business to the hotel.

Saturday 1.5.19—							
Names	Room No.	No. of Guests	Terms	Rate	No. of nights	Date of booking	Notes
Mr & Mrs R. L. Essex	402	2	R+B	£129 p.p.	7	16.3.19—	Arr. 11 a.m. Garage
Miss J. H. Essex	405	1	R+B	£143 p.p.	7	16.3.19—	Arr. 11 a.m.

Figure 3.9 *Hotel bookings diary*

3.4 RESERVATION CHARTS

The types of charts used by the reservations office can vary from hotel to hotel. Groups or chains of hotels usually follow a standard system and use the same type of reservation and room status charts. What is more important is that the reservation office and front desk have an up-to-the-minute visual picture of the room status of the hotel whatever system is used.

Advance reservation — power scan (Fig. 3.10)

This is a manually-operated scan. All the rooms of the hotel, floor by floor are charted on a flat board. A clear white transparency on a roll with all the days and dates of the year at the top, revolves from right to left at the touch of a button. Special coloured marking pens, which can be easily erased when changes are made, are used to block in room allocations. With this type of scan the room reservations for every room for any given day can be brought into view.

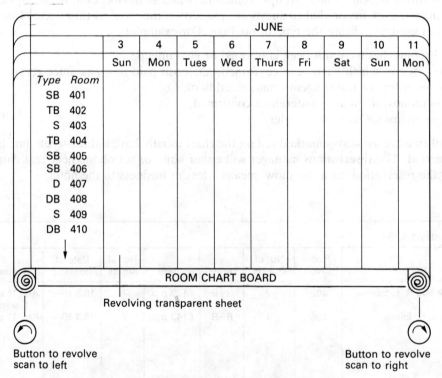

		JUNE								
		3	4	5	6	7	8	9	10	11
		Sun	Mon	Tues	Wed	Thurs	Fri	Sat	Sun	Mon
Type	*Room*									
SB	401									
TB	402									
S	403									
TB	404									
SB	405									
SB	406									
D	407									
DB	408									
S	409									
DB	410									

ROOM CHART BOARD

Revolving transparent sheet

Button to revolve
scan to left

Button to revolve
scan to right

Coloured marking pencils used (easily erased)
KEY: Red — Not confirmed
Green — Confirmed
Yellow — Airline or travel agents guaranteed
Blue — Groups, conferences, seminars
Black — Rooms OOO (out of order).

Figure 3.10 *Advance reservation — power scan*

The conventional chart (Fig. 3.11)

1. This bookings chart covers one calendar month with dates clearly marked at the top and the room numbers and their descriptions at the side. Symbols are sometimes used to indicate the type of room:

Single room	S or (−)
Single room with bath	SB or (−B)
Twin-bedded room	T or (=)
Twin-bedded room with bath	TB or (= B)
Double-bedded room	D or (×)
Double-bedded room with bath	DB or (×B)
Suites	

2. In hotels where bookings are made several months in advance, charts for each month are prepared.
3. Entries are made on the chart as soon as an offer of accommodation has been made. The entries are always in pencil so that they can be easily erased should there be any cancellations or changes in the booking.
4. When a room reservation has been confirmed it is then marked as confirmed on the chart and great care must be taken that all entries are correctly checked and charted.

The chart shows that room 402 has been allocated to R. L. Essex from 1 May to noon, 8 May and room 405 has been allocated to J. Essex (1 guest) from 1 May to noon, 8 May.

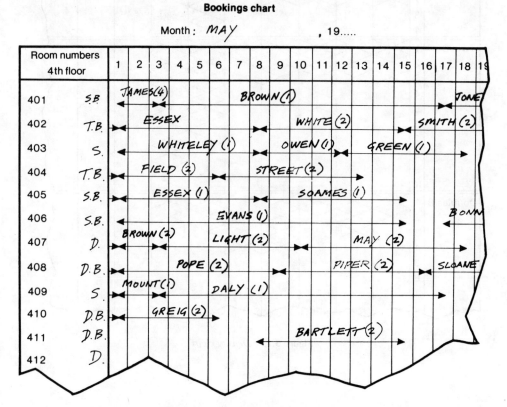

Bookings chart

Month : MAY , 19.....

Figure 3.11 *Conventional reservation chart*

The density chart (Fig. 3.12)

This chart is designed to show at a glance exactly how many rooms have been let and exactly how many rooms are still available to be let and their type. As with the conventional chart, the dates are marked clearly along the top and the rooms in their different categories run from top to bottom. A large hotel with several floors would have a density chart for every floor.

By studying Fig. 3.12 you will observe that:

May 1st 2 singles, 5 twins, 4 doubles are still available for let.
May 2nd 2 singles, 7 twins, 2 doubles are still available for let.
May 3rd 2 singles, 7 twins, 2 doubles are still available for let.
May 4th No singles, 4 twins, 3 doubles are still available for let.
May 5th 2 singles, no twins, 3 doubles are still available for let.

Sometimes a large coloured dot (red for stop) is used to emphasise when there are no rooms available for let in a certain category.

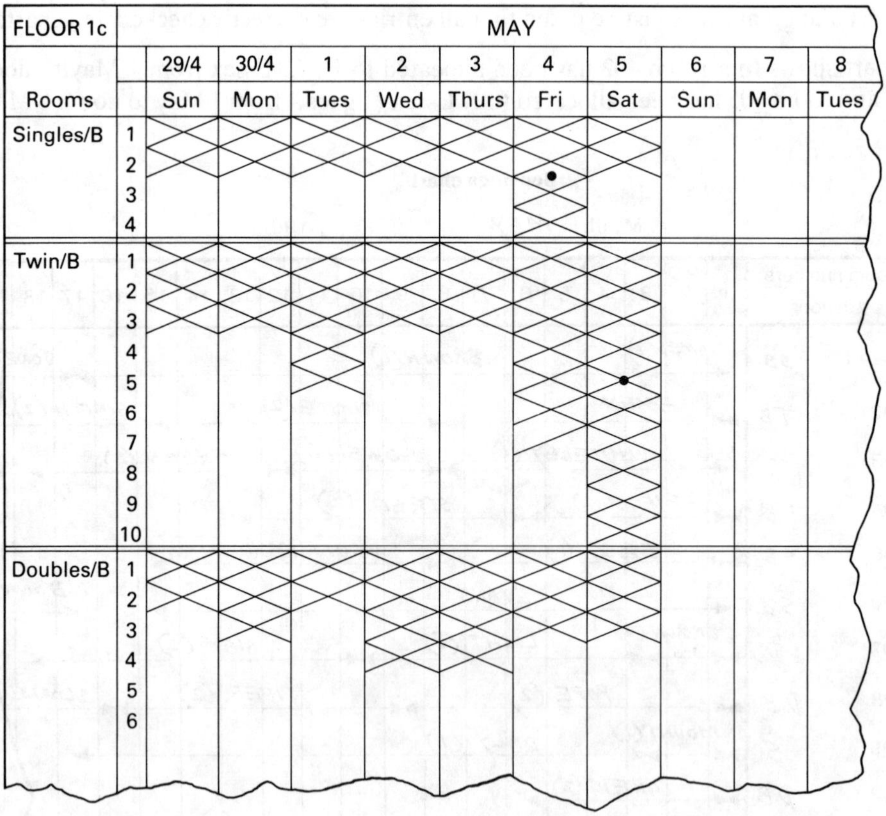

Figure 3.12 *Density chart*

Stop-go charts (Fig. 3.13)

Another type of chart used by large hotels is called a 'stop-go chart'. These are prominently displayed in the reservations area or the reception office and enable the receptionists to see at a glance whether they can accept a booking for a certain date. The chart has a space for each day of the year and symbols are used to indicate the non-availability of the various types of accommodation on certain days.

From the 'stop-go chart' the reservations staff can see at a glance that on Friday 4 May and Saturday 5 May there are no single or double rooms available. On Friday 1 June and Saturday 2 June there are no single or double rooms available. On Monday 2 July, Tuesday 3 July, Wednesday 4 July there are no singles, doubles or suites available as there is a conference in the hotel, and there is no accommodation available on Friday 6 July or Saturday 7 July.

Key: ○ — No singles
　　　□ — No Twins or Doubles
　　　△ — No Suites
　　　//// — Conferences – Tours – Block-bookings – Special Functions

Day	Sunday	Monday	Tuesday	Wednesday	Thursday	Friday	Saturday	Sunday	Monday	Tuesday
Date			1	2	3	4	5	6	7	8
MAY						○□	○□			
Date						1	2	3	4	5
JUNE						○□	○□			
Date	1	2	3	4	5	6	7	8	9	10
JULY		////○□△	////○□△	////○□△		○□△	○□△			

Figure 3.13 *Stop-go chart*

Simultaneous message machine

This machine has a two-station link; a message written on the machine in the reception office will appear simultaneously on the machine in the housekeeping department and vice versa. When a guest checks out, the reception desk staff will write a message on the machine informing the housekeeping department that the room is vacant and needs servicing. When the room has been cleaned the housekeeping department staff will write a message on the machine informing the reception desk that the room is ready for re-letting. This simple device provides instantaneous communication between departments and ensures that the room status board has up-to-the-minute information on the availability of rooms.

Electronic room status boards

Many of the more modern hotels have installed electronic room status boards which link the reception office with the housekeeper and every room. There is a board in the reception office, cashier's office and housekeeper's office with a switch in every bedroom. The system is simple:

1. A green light on the board indicates that the room is vacant and has been serviced and cleaned.
2. A red light on the board indicates that the room is 'on change'.
3. Both lights off indicate that the room is let.

When a guest checks in the receptionist allocates a room showing a green light; he or she presses a switch and the green light goes off on the board as well as on the cashier's and housekeeper's boards. When the guest departs, after settling the account, the cashier will press a switch and the light will go from off to red to indicate that the room is vacant and ready to be cleaned. The housekeeper then has the room serviced and when it is ready for letting, presses the switch in the bedroom which will then show a green light on all boards, indicating that the room is now ready to be let.

The Whitney system (Figs. 3.14 and 3.15)

This is a USA patented system for hotels, whereby the names of guests requesting reservations are typed on four by one and a half inch paper or cardboard and inserted in moveable aluminium pockets (Fig. 3.16) alphabetically under the date of reservation. The night prior to the arrival of guests the section of the rack containing the reservations for that particular day is removed from the advance reservations rack (Fig. 3.15) and placed alongside the room rack (Fig. 3.14) and becomes the current reservation rack. After serving its purpose it is returned to the advance reservation section and used for additional future reservations. These reservation racks replace the booking diary and are used as the 'arrivals list' for each day in conjunction with the reception board.

Figure 3.14 *Room rack (by courtesy of the Whitney Duplicating Check Company, New York)*

Figure 3.15 *Advance and current reservation racks*
(by courtesy of the Whitney Duplicating Check Company, New York)

Room racks (Figs. 3.16 and 3.17)

The Whitney rack system is planned exactly as the advance reservations. There are racks for each floor containing an aluminium pocket for each room in vertical number order. Details of the type of the room, rates and equipment remain permanently in the rack. Details of the guests occupying the room are typed on a slip and inserted in the room pocket. The system provides several different types of room racks with innovations and signals that can provide information for the receptionists; for example, pockets can have a centre window with two-colour sliding signals which can be moved to show red when the room has been assigned, yellow when the room is 'on change' and clear when the room is ready for letting.

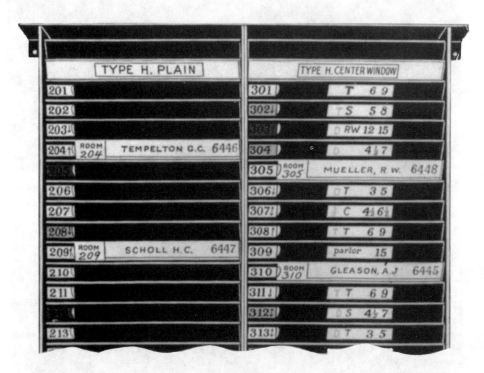

Figure 3.16 *Room racks (by courtesy of the Whitney Duplicating Check Company, New York)*

Figure 3.17 *Combination room and key and pocket racks*
(by courtesy of the Whitney Duplicating Check Company, New York)

The reception board (Fig. 3.18)

There are many different designs of reception board used in hotels but whatever the style the purpose is the same: to provide the receptionist with up-to-the-minute information on the status of every room. The board is usually angled in the reception office in such a manner that it is entirely out of view of the guest but visible at all times to the receptionist. The board is arranged horizontally so that each tier represents a floor. There is a slot for each room and the names of the occupants, dates of arrival and departure and terms are typed on a card or slip and placed in the appropriate room number slot. Coloured cards or strips can be used to indicate whether a room is vacant, occupied by staff, being cleaned or out of commission.

As the reception board can only show the accommodation position for one day, the conventional and density charts are still necessary for selling accommodation in advance.

Airline and travel agents guaranteed reservations

Large transient hotels very often enter into agreements with certain airlines or travel agents whereby they will hold a number of rooms specifically for them on a guarantee basis. This means that the airlines or travel agents guarantee to pay for those rooms whether they are used by their clients or not. If they wish to cancel any of the rooms allocated they must do so within the time limit set by the hotel or they will be billed for them. A typical example of this type of agreement is when an airport hotel will hold a set number of rooms for the airline pilots and stewards/stewardesses who have stop-overs between flights.

Travel agents often advertise package tours which include a stay at a certain hotel. When this is the case the travel agent will have an agreement with the hotel to reserve the number of rooms required for their package tour clients.

The hotel will send the bill for accommodation used, direct to the airline or travel agents. Meals and drinks are usually paid for separately by the guest unless it is included in the package agreement.

Central reservation systems

Large groups of hotels which are linked by computer usually operate their own central reservation system. Information on the availability of accommodation within the chain of hotels is fed into the computer and by telephoning the central reservation number the customer can be directed to the location and type of hotel which is able to meet their requirements.

Similarly, other centralised reservation systems are in operation which are not attached to any particular group. They work on a commission basis. Hotels that wish to join the scheme provide details of their location, accommodation and facilities. The information is fed into a computer so that when an inquiry is made to the centralised reservation service number the customer can be directed to the hotels with the available type of accommodation in the area they require.

In order that the scheme functions efficiently it is essential that the reception offices of the hotels within the scheme inform central reservations of the up-to-the-minute availability of rooms to let at all times; failure to do this could result in double-bookings, loss of goodwill and unnecessary charges being levied against the hotel for the service.

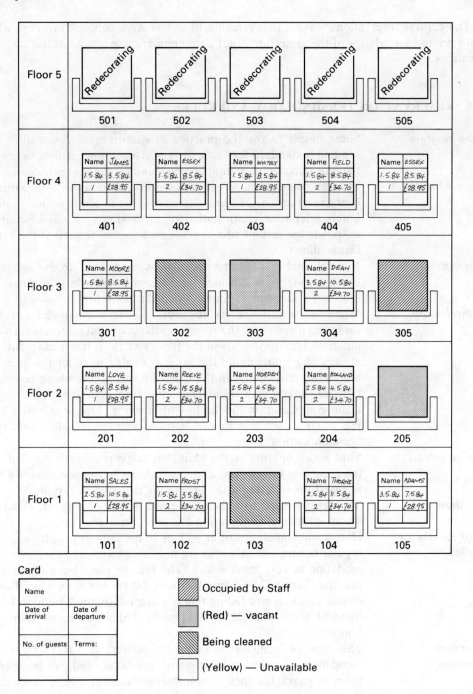

Floor 5	Redecorating	Redecorating	Redecorating	Redecorating	Redecorating
	501	502	503	504	505

Floor 4:
- 401 — Name: JAMES, 1.5.84 / 3.5.84, 1 / £28.95
- 402 — Name: ESSEX, 1.5.84 / 8.5.84, 2 / £34.70
- 403 — Name: WHITELY, 1.5.84 / 8.5.84, 1 / £28.95
- 404 — Name: FIELD, 1.5.84 / 8.5.84, 2 / £34.70
- 405 — Name: ESSEX, 1.5.84 / 8.5.84, 1 / £28.95

Floor 3:
- 301 — Name: MOORE, 1.5.84 / 8.5.84, 1 / £28.95
- 302 — Being cleaned
- 303 — vacant
- 304 — Name: DEAN, 3.5.84 / 10.5.84, 2 / £34.70
- 305 — Occupied by Staff

Floor 2:
- 201 — Name: LOVE, 1.5.84 / 8.5.84, 1 / £28.95
- 202 — Name: REEVE, 1.5.84 / 15.5.84, 2 / £34.70
- 203 — Name: NORDEN, 2.5.84 / 4.5.84, 2 / £34.70
- 204 — Name: HOLLAND, 2.5.84 / 4.5.84, 2 / £34.70
- 205 — vacant

Floor 1:
- 101 — Name: SALES, 2.5.84 / 10.5.84, 1 / £28.95
- 102 — Name: FROST, 1.5.84 / 3.5.84, 2 / £34.70
- 103 — Occupied by Staff
- 104 — Name: THORNE, 2.5.84 / 11.5.84, 2 / £34.70
- 105 — Name: ADAMS, 3.5.84 / 7.5.84, 1 / £28.95

Card

Name	
Date of arrival	Date of departure
No. of guests	Terms:

Legend:
- Occupied by Staff
- (Red) — vacant
- Being cleaned
- (Yellow) — Unavailable

Figure 3.18 *Reception board*

The central reservations service is invaluable to overseas visitors or travellers who have limited knowledge of the areas and hotel accommodation available in the various localities.

3.5 RESERVATION TERMINOLOGY AND RULES

Confirmation	Some hotels follow the practice of confirming a reservation by sending a standard letter or card which acknowledges a deposit, the type of accommodation reserved and garage space if necessary.
No confirmation	In large transient hotels it is not practical to confirm in writing every reservation, as guests come and go at short notice. Some hotels telephone confirmation of a booking and will of course acknowledge receipt of a deposit or a special request if the time factor allows.
Deposits	Non-returnable deposits are usually requested from overseas visitors booking in advance, and resort hotels whose business is seasonal also usually request a deposit to confirm a booking.
Cancellations	When a cancellation is received the reservation has to be cancelled throughout the system, in the diary and reservation chart and noted on documents in the filing system. If it is a cancellation at very short notice and the hotel is unable to re-let the accommodation, particularly in the case of resort hotels whose reservations are taken well in advance, the hotel may then be able to claim compensation for the loss of business. Transient hotels are less likely to suffer a loss of business and can usually re-let the accommodation.
6 p.m. release	Most hotels operate on the basis that unless previously notified by the guest that they will be a late arrival, the accommodation will be released for reletting if the guest fails to arrive by 6 p.m.
No show	This term is used to indicate the non-arrival of a guest, and for whom no formal cancellation has been received.
T or P (take or place)	Hotels will sometimes offer a 'T or P' booking to people, usually regular business clients who are only able to reserve their accommodation at very short notice. The take or place booking means that the client will be offered a room if there has been a 'no show' or cancellation, and failing that accommodation will be found for them at a comparable hotel, usually within the same chain of hotels.
Guaranteed arrival	This type of facility is usually only offered to travel agents or companies who deal regularly with the hotel, and can be relied upon to guarantee their commitment. Payment will be made for the accommodation reserved whether the guest arrives or not. This type of guarantee will reverse the 6 p.m. release procedure and is useful for overseas travellers whose times of arrival are governed by their air, sea or rail travel arrangements.
VIPs or CIPs	Reservations for very important persons or commercially important persons are usually dealt with by senior members of the

	management. If special arrangements have to be made a note in the diary will remind the duty manager when VIPs or CIPs are due to arrive.
Special commission bookings	Reservations made through travel agents, tour operators or certain companies are usually subject to special rates and commissions. A note is usually made in the diary to this effect to remind the reception desk.
Hotel discount card	This card costs approximately twelve pounds p.a. and entitles holders to a ten per cent discount on accommodation.
Back to back reservations	Travel agents and tour operators often make back to back reservations which means that certain accommodation is booked over a period of time and as one group of guests depart another group takes their place.
A & TO	This is an accommodation and taxi order. This is a voucher issued by airlines when travellers have been delayed in transit. It is issued to passengers whose flights have been cancelled or delayed and is redeemable by the airlines at face value. It usually covers the cost of accommodation, breakfast, a main meal and return taxi fare from airport to hotel.
Lead time	The time between the booking date and the arrival date.
Chance	No previous reservation with the hotel.
Stay on	A guest who extends his/her stay beyond the original reservation date.
Early departure	A guest who checks out before his/her scheduled departure date.
Room nights	Number of rooms available × the period of time covered by reservations chart — a principle of reservations charts to show the number of room nights available.

3.6 TRAVEL AGENTS, TOURS AND GROUPS

Today most people rely on travel agents to make their travel arrangements and book their accommodation. Tour operators organise and plan package holidays and tours and specialist organisations plan conferences and group travel for other organisations. These agents work on a commission basis and special rates and discounts are negotiated with the hotel groups and will depend on several factors:

(a) the amount of business guaranteed by the agents during both high season and low season;
(b) the time of the year;
(c) the time of the week;
(d) the numbers in the group;
(e) the accommodation required;
(f) other facilities required.

Not all hotels will accept package holidays or tour groups. Luxury hotels may only allocate twenty per cent of their accommodation, whereas other hotels may regard this type of business as their main source of income and allocate eighty per cent or more of their accommodation and plan their services around this kind of market.

Tour booking

When handling tour bookings details must be thoroughly discussed with the agents before the group's expected arrival, for example, whether the baggage handling and tips are to be included in the rates and the methods of payment for extras by the guests.

Group booking form (Fig. 3.19)

This is a reservation for the group to be completed by the tour operator giving full details from which the hotel will be able to organise all the services required.

Confirmation and room list

It is usual for the hotel to have a cancellation deadline usually four weeks before the expected arrival date. Any cancellation after that date will be charged at full non-arrival rate. When finalising arrangements and confirming the reservation the tour operator will usually include a rooming list giving full names of all the group, their nationality and passport numbers and any special requirements such as family groupings or adjacent rooms.

GROUP BOOKING FORM   No.

Group No. ....   Tour Operator ....

Group Leader ....   Telephone No. ....

Number in Group ....   Telex No. ....

Arrival Date ....Time ....

Departure Date ....Time ....

Accommodation			Meals			
Rooms	No.	Rate	Breakfast	Lunch	Afternoon Tea	Dinner
SB TB DB Suites Other						
Special requirements						
Subject to terms and conditions overleaf						

Figure 3.19 *Group booking form*

Registration

1. Groups can register in the usual way when they arrive, each individual completing a separate registration form. With large groups, however, this method can cause chaos at the reception desk.
2. Individual registration forms could be dispensed with and a list of names, initials, nationality and passport numbers could be handed in by the tour operator. This method is not exactly reliable as the information given could not be accurate and there are no individual signatures of the members of the group, which could cause problems when billing the guests for any extras.
3. Individual registration forms could be given to the tour operator for completion by the guests en route to the hotel; it is then a simple matter of handling the registration forms at reception on arrival.

Arrival of groups

The arrival of large groups of people at the same time will always mean pressure on the reception staff, hall porters and other departments. If a group arrives in the morning before the housekeeping department has had time to clean and service all the rooms, then the group must be made comfortable whilst waiting to gain access to their rooms. The head porter will have the responsibility of organising parking spaces for the coaches, seeing that the luggage is unloaded, counted, checked and agreed with the group leader and dispatched to the rooms as quickly as possible.

Account charges

Details of what is included in the rate to be charged to the tour operators, such as meals, beverages and gratuities, will have been discussed and finalised between the tour operator and the hotel before confirmation of the reservation.

It is usual for a group account to be opened and a separate account for the individual guest also to be opened. Any extra charges the guest incurs will be charged to their room number, and the account settled personally by them on check-out. To avoid having a large number of small accounts in the ledger it is often the case in some hotels to ask members of groups or parties to pay for 'extras' at time of service.

A tour operator voucher will have been sent to the hotel with the confirmation and room list. On check-out the group leader will hand the reception manager a copy of this voucher detailing all the charges the tour operator will be responsible for and signed for by the group leader. The two copies of the voucher and the hotel's account will be married together, thoroughly checked and authorised by the reception manager, then forwarded to the tour operator or travel agent for payment.

Departure of groups

Like the arrival of a big group, the departure can be equally chaotic. It requires organisation and planning, as one group usually follows another and for the changeover to be smooth all departments must be working to maximum efficiency. Guests will be required to vacate their rooms by 11 a.m., noon at the latest, to enable the housekeeping staff to service and clean rooms for the next group. If a group is not leaving until the afternoon it is advisable to have a hospitality room available for luggage to be stored and for guests to have access to toilet facilities.

The billing office must ensure that all 'extras' are charged to the correct accounts and bills settled before luggage can be moved, and finally that all room keys are collected.

Group bookings, tours, conferences

When a hotel receives an enquiry for an 'en bloc' reservations, which means that a number of rooms have to be reserved to accommodate a group of people, it is essential that the reservations charts are studied carefully. If the hotel accepts too many block bookings that could possibly result in the loss of other reservations from clients who may return to the hotel on regular basis. To avoid this, research work is done and the hotel decides how many of this type of booking they can accept.

3.7 OVERBOOKING

It is the aim of any hotel to achieve the maximum room occupancy and one must remember that a 'sleeper' lost (bed unoccupied) is a financial loss that cannot be regained. Therefore, many hotels work on the principle of accepting a percentage more reservations than there is accommodation available. A calculation is made of the percentage of non-arrivals, cancellations and guests that terminate their stay earlier than expected. For example:

$$\frac{\text{Non-arrivals} - \text{Cancellations} - \text{Early departures}}{\text{Rooms reserved}}$$

$$\frac{16}{200} \times \frac{100}{1} = 8\%$$

Overbooking allowed: 8% of total number of rooms

$$\frac{8}{100} \times 300 = 24 \text{ rooms}$$

This figure is noted on the reservation charts and means that the reception office will accept that number of reservations above their maximum accommodation. If the unexpected happens and the hotel is completely full and they have overbooked then it is the responsibility of the hotel to find alternate accommodation of the same standard at another hotel for the overflow and bear any additional costs (cf. transporting guests).

3.8 CHECK-IN OF GUESTS

When the guest arrives he/she should have their confirmation slips, airline or travel agents voucher as evidence of their reservation. These are checked against the hotel's records. If no confirmation slip has been sent the receptionist would check the reservation. In the case of a walk-in or chance guest then the room status board would be checked to see if accommodation was available.

Checking credit-worthiness

As it takes approximately three or four days to clear a personal cheque, more hotels are adopting the policy of only accepting personal cheques for payments in advance, or with seven day's notice if payment of the bill is to be made by cheque. Payment by cheque will be accepted if accompanied by a banker's card (see Chapter 5) and if it is within the limit of the banker's card (usually £50).

Credit card approval

Credit cards are now being regarded as a more acceptable method of settling accounts as the credit card companies guarantee settlement of the bill up to the credit limit of their clients (see Chapter 5). If a guest has indicated that he/she intends to settle by credit card, on arrival of the guest the credit card is requested and an imprint of the card is taken and signed by the guest. The hotel can then telephone the central number of the credit card companies and request the approval code as to the credit-worthiness of the card holder. If the credit approval is declined then the management contacts the guest immediately. If guests have no credit cards they are usually asked to prepay for their stay at the hotel and all incidentals in bars and restaurants etc. are on a cash basis.

Many hotels now have a credit card microphone machine, which is linked to a central computer serving the five major credit card companies, i.e. Visa, American Express, Diners Club, Carte Blanche, Mastercard (see Chapter 5). By putting the card into the machine an approval or disapproval code number will be shown on the visual digital screen.

Identity booklets (Fig. 3.20)

It is now common practice in large hotels to issue guests on arrival with identity booklets in attractively designed folders containing information on the facilities available in the hotel. The booklets are also designed to advertise and highlight features of the hotel. The name of the guest, room number and key code number which, for security reasons, is different from the room number are printed inside. If the guest is settling the bill by credit card they can avail themselves of the express check-out service.

Specially coloured booklets are used for VIP guests or regular users of the hotel and carry added privileges such as preregistration, express check-in, special rates, welcome cocktails, daily newspapers and other complimentary features.

Receiving and registering guests

The law requires that guests must register with the hotel (see Chapter 8). Some small hotels still maintain a hotel register in either book form or (Fig. 3.21) with loose leaves. The majority of hotels now use the printed registration forms (Fig. 3.8) because of their many advantages:

1. They are neat, legible, easily handled and can be filed in chronological order.
2. The information on them is confidential and therefore it ensures that guests only see their own forms.
3. In the case of a group booking, or a rapid succession of arrivals many guests can be completing their registration forms at the same time.

FRONT

BACK

TELEPHONE DIRECTORY

GUEST SERVICES
ASSISTANCE INFORMATION
1250

ASSISTANT MANAGER	1297
HEAD PORTER	1365
FRONT OFFICE	1271
HOUSEKEEPING	1285
ROOM SERVICE	1291
WAKE-UP SERVICE	0
PAPILLON RESTAURANT	1273
TARTAN BAR	1274
'JINGLES' NIGHT CLUB	1276
ROOM RESERVATIONS	1180
TOURS AND TRANSPORTATION	1257
THEATRE TICKETS	1257

THE

GRAND

HOTEL
* * * *

FOLD

FOLD

Tel. 0323–12345

INSIDE

* * * * WELCOME TO THE GRAND HOTEL * * * *

If you presented a credit card upon check-in simply fill out the information below and leave this
card at the front desk on the day of your departure, without standing in line.

Your account will be processed through your credit card and if you desire we will send you an
itemised statement immediately upon your departure.

Fold
over

EXPRESS CHECK OUT

Signature ....

I plan to leave at ....on ....
                             time   date

☐ I will *not* require an itemised statement
☐ Please send a copy of my hotel account to:

NAME ....

ADDRESS .... POSTAL CODE...............................

GUEST NAME ....

ROOM No.   KEY CODE No.

PLEASE LEAVE THIS CARD AT FRONT DESK ON DAY OF DEPARTURE

Figure 3.20 *Identity booklets*

Hotel register					
Sheet number 121				Date 1 May 1984	
Name	Town, county	Nationality	Room number	Time of arrival	Car registration number
Mr ROY LEONARD ESSEX	LONDON SW 1	BRITISH	402	11.15am	TLD 232 R
Mrs JEAN MARION ESSEX	LONDON SW1	BRITISH	402	11.15am	"
Miss JANE HILARY ESSEX	LONDON SW1	BRITISH	405	11.15am	"

Figure 3.21   *Hotel register — book form*

4. International hotels can produce the registration card in several languages, which is of assistance to foreign travellers.
5. The registration forms can easily be checked against the original reservation.

When receiving guests the procedure is as follows:

1. On arrival the guests are assisted with the luggage by the hall porter, who will escort them to the reception counter.
2. The receptionist welcomes the guests with a smile and greeting, hands the pen to them and asks if they will kindly complete the registration form (Fig. 3.8) or sign the hotel register (Fig. 3.21).
3. The registration is checked to see if it has been correctly completed.
4. The identity booklet (or key card) together with any messages or letters that may be waiting for them are handed to the guest. The room key is given to the porter, who will escort the guest to the room. In the case of a group checking-in the keys, identity booklets or key cards and information sheets are put in individual envelopes for distribution by the group leader.
5. The receptionist should point out to the guest the location of the restaurants, lounges, public rooms and emergency exits and enquire whether there is anything the guest may require or need to know.
6. If possible, either the hall porter or receptionist will escort the guests to their room offering to carry any hand luggage and walking a few steps ahead to open any doors.
7. The escort should preceed the guest into the room, make a quick check to ensure that the room is in order, then hand the key to the guest.

8.   Any electrical appliances should be pointed out to the guests with instructions on use if necessary. The escort should then enquire if they can be of any further service.
9.   The number of pieces of heavy luggage the guest has on arrival should be entered into the luggage book (Fig. 3.22), which is usually kept at the hall porter's desk.
10. The room number should be ticked off on the arrivals and departures list and the guests' names entered on the tabular ledger and their bills started.

Luggage book

Name	Room number	Arrival	Departure	Number of pieces of luggage
Mr & Mrs. R.L. ESSEX	402	1.5.84	8.5.84	2 SUITCASES, 1 VANITY CASE
Miss J.H. ESSEX	405	1.5.84	8.5.84	1 SUITCASE, 1 VANITY CASE

Figure 3.22   *Luggage book*

Aliens (Fig. 3.23)

An alien (foreign national) in addition must register (the Immigration Hotel Records Order 1972):

(a)   the number of his or her passport or registration certificate or other documents establishing the identity or nationality of the alien;
(b)   the date of departure and the next address if known.

If there is any doubt about the passport or other identifying documents advice can always be obtained from the police.

Overseas
visitors/aliens

Passport number

Place of issue

Next destination

Date of departure

Figure 3.23   *Aliens form*

3.9 VALUABLES FOR SAFE-KEEPING

The hotel has a strict liability for the property the guest may bring into the hotel (see Chapter 8) and is obliged to accept valuables such as money, jewellery, furs, etc. for safe-keeping. A special receipt book in triplicate is kept for the purpose. The top copy is given as a receipt to the guest, the second copy remaining in the receipt book, and the third copy is attached to the parcel or valuable concerned. Full details must be entered on the receipt (Fig. 3.24). If a guest deposits a jewel case it must be locked; loose money should be counted and descriptions of individual items should be exact. If a guest wishes to deposit a sealed item, they should sign across the seal and the description 'one sealed envelope' should be written on the receipt.

When guests wish to withdraw from the safe deposit the original receipt must be produced and they must sign the receipt book as proof that they have received back the valuables. If for any reason the original receipt cannot be produced positive proof of identification must be produced before any deposits can be handed over. If a guest wishes to redeposit valuables a new receipt must be issued every time.

An estimated value of the articles is sometimes requested in order that the hotel can be adequately covered by insurance.

RECEIPT FOR VALUABLES		No. 123
GRAND HOTEL **WESTBOURNE** ********		
Name *R.L. ESSEX* Room No. *402*		Date *1.5.1984*
Description		Guests estimated value
1 Locked Jewel Case		*£200=*
1 Sealed envelope		
Guest's signature *R.L. Essex.*	Received by *R. Jones*	
Date returned	Guest's signature	

Figure 3.24 *Receipt for valuables deposited*

Safe deposit boxes

Many large hotels provide individual safe deposit boxes or wall safes for the use of their guests. The models and types may vary, but usually the guest is given one key to the box for which a signature is requested, and the particulars are recorded in a key receipt book. The cashier holds the other key and the safe deposit box can only be opened if both locks are operated at the same time. This is a security precaution against an unauthorised person or the cashier alone being able to open the box.

3.10 LETTER AND KEY RACKS (Fig. 3.25)

In many hotels letter and key racks are located in the hall porter's enquiry office. However, in smaller hotels they are usually located in the reception office. The rack consists of a number of pigeon holes large enough to hold mail of normal size, with a key hook above. Each pigeon hole is clearly numbered by floor and by room. It is used to distribute incoming letters, small packages, and any messages for guests, and it also provides a definite place for keys not in use.

Keys

Master keys, which open all doors, are kept by certain senior members of staff such as the head housekeeper and head porter, and there are usually two keys for every bedroom. The first set of keys is handed to the guest on arrival and the second set is kept on a duplicate key board under the strict supervision of either the head receptionist or

Figure 3.25 *Combined key and letter rack (Wilcox International Inc.)*

head porter. It should be drawn to the attention of the guest that it is desirable that they hand in the keys if they go out and collect them from the enquiry or reception desk on their return. When keys are returned care must be taken to see that they are placed on the correct key hook. By looking at the key rack it is easy to see, if the key is there, that the guest is out of the room or that the room is vacant. If the key is not on the hook then the guest is in. Constant checks should be made on the key rack, usually late at night or early in the morning, so that if any keys go astray the matter is investigated immediately.

Electronic key system (Fig. 3.26)

To overcome the problem of missing and lost keys and keys not being handed back by the guest on departure and to combat the problem of security by which unauthorised persons obtain keys to rooms, many hotels are going to the expense of installing keyless locks on their rooms. This is an electronic system whereby upon arrival the guest is issued with a plastic key card (see Fig. 3.26). A computerised console in the reception office punches holes on the key card. These holes indicate a code of which there are at least four billion combinations in the system. There is no room number on the key card and only the correct code punched on the card will operate and open the room door. If a guest loses a key card or another guest takes over the room a new key card with new code punch holes is issued. The old key card code is invalidated on the computer console and only the new key card code will operate and open the room door.

Figure 3.26 *Electronic key system*

Date 1st May 19—

ARRIVALS

Room number	Type	No. of Guests Adults	No. of Guests Children	Name	No. of nights	Time of arrival	Notes
402	TB	2		ESSEX, M|Ms. R.L.	7	11.00	Garage
405	SB	1		ESSEX, Miss J.H.	7	11.00	
406	SB	1		EVANS, Mrs R.J.	14	14.00	
410	DB	2		GREIG, M|Ms J.L.	5	14.00	
401	SB	1		JAMES, Mr. A.	2	15.00	
201	SB	1		LOVE, Ms. Y.	7	15.00	
407	D	2		LOWIN, M|Ms S.T.	2	12.00	
301	SB	1		MOORE, Mr. T.	14	12.00	
409	S	1		MOUNT, Mr. K.	5	14.00	
404	TB	2		MOSTYN, M|Ms L.	2	14.00	
102	TB	2	1	PITT, M|Ms.Miss R.	2	16.00	Cot/Garage
408	DB	2		POPE, M|Ms. R.	8	16.30	Garage
202	TB	2		REEVE, M|Mr. S.	14	14.30	Garage
209	TB	Change of room		YEW, M|Ms. T.	7	11.30	*
403	S	1		WHITELY, Miss J.	7	13.30	
15		21	1				

DEPARTURES

Room number	Type	No. of Guests Adults	No. of Guests Children	Name	Time of departure	Notes
103	TB	Change of room		YEW, M|Ms. T.	11.30	*
105	SB	1		WILLIAMS, Mrs. B.	08.00	
110	TB	1	1	MURRAY, Mr/Master	09.00	
205	SB	1		MARTIN, Mr. A.	09.00	
209	TB	1	1	OWEN, Ms|s	08.00	
302	TB	1	1	WHITE, M|s L.	11.00	
305	SB	1		SULLIVAN, Ms	11.00	
307	SB	1		STEWART, Mr. A.	09.30	
402	TB	1	1	SMITH, Ms|s	08.00	
404	TB	2		KYLE, M|Ms	11.00	
405	SB	1		BROWN, Miss L.	09.00	
407	D	2		LEWIS, M|Ms. J.	09.30	
408	DB	2		POWELL, M|Ms. T.	08.00	
409	S	1		DOUGLAS, Ms. A.	10.00	
410	DB	2		DOUGLAS, M|Ms.	10.00	
15		18	4			

Figure 3.27 Arrivals and departures list

3.11 THE ARRIVALS AND DEPARTURES LISTS (Fig. 3.27)

It is essential that all departments are notified in advance of guests due to arrive and those due to depart. The housekeeping departments has to ensure that all rooms are prepared for the new arrivals and when a room is vacated the chambermaids have to change the linen and clean the room ready for the next letting. The restaurant manager has to know the estimated number of guests to be expected in the restaurant and in order to prepare the meals the chef needs to be informed of any special requirements. Arrivals and departures lists are prepared daily in advance and copies circulated to all departments.

Arrivals list

This list is prepared one day in advance from the reservations records. It is in alphabetical order and shows rooms allocated, name, number of nights' stay, number of guests, estimated times of arrival and any special requirements. If the Whitney system is used the arrivals list can be prepared from the arrival rack.

Notification slips (Figs. 3.28, 3.29)

As the arrivals list is only made up from guests who have made reservations in advance, it will not show 'chance' guests or a guest who changes rooms after the list has been circulated. As room status information must be up-to-the-minute, notification slips are circulated immediately to all departments should a 'chance' arrival or sudden change of room, or any other eventuality make it necessary to inform all departments, so that any action required can be taken.

ARRIVAL NOTICE No. 135	Distribution	
Date 1st. May 19— Time 14.00 hrs.	Manager	✓
	Billing office	✓
Name Mr. G. James Room No. 107	Cashier	✓
No. of nights 2 Rate £21.	Head porter	✓
	Telephone	✓
No. of sleepers 1 Terms R+B	Housekeeper	✓
Notes 'Chance'	Restaurant manager	✓
	Bars manager	✓
	Room service	✓
Signature G.M. Paige		

Figure 3.28 *Arrival notice*

Room change	No. 272	Distribution	
		Manager	✓
Date .....1ˢᵗ· May 19 — Time .....15.00 hⱽˢ.		Billing office	✓
Name .....M/s LOWIN S.T. From Room No. 407		Cashier	✓
No. of nights .....2 To Room No. 302		Head porter	✓
		Telephone	✓
No. of sleepers .....2 Rate .....£19 :		Housekeeper	✓
Terms .....R + B		Restaurant manager	✓
Notes .....Double for Twin		Bars manager	✓
		Room service	✓
Signature G.M. Paige			

Figure 3.29 *Room change*

Chance guests

Chance visitors are those that arrive without previous reservation. If a guest has no luggage, payment in advance is usually requested. If, however, a chance guest with luggage can produce credit cards and identification, no deposit is asked for. Tact must always be used when asking for identification or payment in advance.

Change of room

If a guest wishes to change rooms and his or her arrival has already been entered on the arrivals list, the change of room must be treated as a departure from one room and an arrival in another room. As the change of room will have no effect on the number of guests staying in the hotel, no entry is made in the column showing number of guests (Fig. 3.27). If the arrivals and departures list has already been circulated, a change of room notification slip must be sent to all departments informing them of the room change.

Departure lists

The departure list is prepared by the reception office and circulated to all heads of departments in order that:

1. The housekeeper can plan the work rotas to ensure that all rooms will be checked, cleaned and serviced ready for re-let, as soon as they have been vacated.
2. The hall porter will be able to organise his or her staff to handle the luggage for departing guests.

			Royal Hotel					
			London					
			****				Date 7.5.19—	
Mr. T. Jones							Room 403	

Date	May 1	May 2	May 3	May 4	May 5	May 6	May 7	Total
Accommodation	40.00	40.00	40.00	40.00	40.00	40.00	40.00	280.00
Early Morning Beverage	.50	.50	.50	.50	.50	.50	.50	3.50
Breakfast	3.00	3.00	3.00	3.00	3.00	3.00	3.00	21.00
Luncheon			6.75		6.75			13.50
Afternoon								
Dinner	8.20			7.40				15.60
Drinks	1.40		1.10	1.10		1.50		5.10
Telephone	2.50	1.00			3.00			6.50
Newspaper	.40	.40	.40	.40	.40	.40		2.40
Sundries								
Visitors' Paid Out	Taxi 4.00							4.00
Daily Total	60.00	44.90	51.75	52.40	53.65	45.40	43.50	351.60
Brought Forward	—	60.00	104.90	156.65	209.05	262.70	308.10	
Total	60.00	104.90	156.65	209.05	262.70	308.10	351.60	351.60
Cash Received								
Deposits/Allownaces								50.00
Amount due								301.60

Figure 3.30 *Copy of guest's bill*

3. All other departments will check that charging vouchers have been forwarded to the billing office for entry on the guest's folio (Fig. 3.8(c) Fig. 3.30) before the guest departs.

Should there be an unexpected early departure of a guest, a notification slip is circulated to all departments immediately, informing them of the name and room number of the departing guest.

Procedures for departures

1. The billing office will check that all charges and payments made have been posted to the guest's account and have it prepared ready to present to the guest for settlement.

2. The cashier will ensure that all valuables in the safe or in a safety deposit box are collected by the guest and a signed receipt obtained.
3. The head porter will have staff ready to handle any luggage. Some hotels give a luggage clearance pass to the head porter when the account has been settled. The head porter will check off his or her departure list when luggage is cleared.
4. The head housekeeper will tick off his or her departure list when the room has been checked and cleared.
5. The account is settled, keys are handed in and the guest departs with a warm invitation to 'please come again'.

The reception office will then amend their records as follows:

1. The guest's name card will be removed from the reception board (Fig. 3.18).
2. The name strip is removed from the guest's alphabetical list (Fig. 3.32).
3. Date of departure is noted on the room history card (Fig. 3.33).
4. If a guest history card is kept it will brought up to date (Fig. 3.35).
5. If a mail forwarding form (see Fig. 6.2) has been completed it will be filed alphabetically.

Daily summary sheets (Fig. 3.31)

Daily summary sheets are prepared for management and other heads of department. These are for information, for cross-checking purposes, and for statistics.

DAILY SUMMARY		DATE 1·5.19-	Distribution to:	
No. of Rooms	Details	No. of Sleepers	Manager	✓
			Asst/manager	✓
33	Guests in residence last night	46	Housekeeper	✓
15	Departures	22	Restaurant manager	✓
			Head porter	✓
18	Sub-total	24	Billing office	✓
15	Arrivals	21	Cashier	✓
2	Chance	4	Notes	
33	Guests in residence tonight	49	Room 107 } chance Room 302	
Signature	J. Chambers		HEAD RECEPTIONIST.	

Figure 3.31 *Daily summary sheet*

3.12 BASIC RECEPTION DUTIES IN THE AVERAGE-SIZED HOTEL

A large percentage of the hotel industry consists of small or medium-sized hotels where manual systems are still operated. In these hotels the receptionist duties are many and varied. Apart from receiving and registering guests, making reservations, dealing with enquiries and maintaining records, the following tasks have to be dealt with:

Morning duties

1. Check the night shift log book for any messages or matters to be dealt with.
2. The post has to be sorted, letters attached to previous correspondence and any mail requiring attention dealt with or distributed to the appropriate department.
3. Cash floats, which are the set sums of money handed out to the restaurants and bars in order to provide them with change to start the day's business, are checked, ready for collection by the departmental heads.
4. Any late night arrivals must be entered on the previous days tabular ledger (see Chapter 5) and the guest's folio (bill) started. The tabular ledger is then balanced and closed, and a daily summary sheet completed.
5. Early morning teas, telephone calls, newspapers and any other visitors' charge slips or paid-outs must be entered on the current tabular ledger and guests' folios.
6. All bills for departing guests must be made up and double checked to ensure that all charges have been posted to them (Fig. 3.8(c), Fig. 3.30).
7. Correspondence relating to reservations and arrivals is checked.
8. Menus have to be typed and duplicated.
9. The cash book (see Chapter 5) is written up and balanced.
10. Cash is counted and prepared for paying into the bank (see Chapter 5).
11. During the morning checks should be made on guests scheduled for a noon departure who have not yet settled their accounts.
12. A midday balance should be struck on the tabular ledger.
13. Any luncheon checks, lounge drinks and room service checks are posted to the tabular ledger and entered on guests' folios.
14. Before the brigade of receptionists change shift they must ensure that all work has been processed as far as possible and that any messages or matters to be dealt with are brought to the attention of the evening shift.
15. Incident book (log book)
    Most hotels keep an incident book or log book to record any unusual happenings during the course of the day. It is not necessary to write a long report of each happening but the essential details such as date, time, detail and signature of person making the entry. An example would be:

July 1	Mr Jones, Room 112, complained of too much noise coming from
Time 8 am	Room 110, asked to change rooms. Transferred to Room 120. All departments notified (signature).
Time 1200	Mrs Brown, Room 108, wishes to extend her stay for two nights July 7 and 8. Please inform her if a room will be available for that date (signature).

Evening duties

1. Cash floats should be rechecked to ensure that cashiers have enough change for the evening business.
2. Any new arrivals should be dealt with as they come in and guests' folios started.
3. Any correspondence or filing left over from the morning shift should be dealt with.
4. Any charges for luncheons, afternoon teas and dinners should be posted as far as possible to the tabular ledger and the guests' bills.
5. Any purchases invoices should be checked and entered into the purchases day book and the ledger.
6. The arrivals and departures list for the next day should be typed and copies distributed to all departments.
7. A final check balance on the tabular ledger should be made. If machine accounting is used, the roll should be taken out of the machine, the date changed and all totals checked to make sure that they are at zero.
8. Check housekeeper's lists (room vacancy list (see Chapter 7, Fig. 7.2)) to note rooms available for letting.
9. Write up night porter's book and notify him or her of rooms available for letting and any late arrivals, their names and room numbers.
10. Prepare the manager's report on daily turnover and rooms occupied.
11. Prepare new tabular ledger.
12. Check all cash received from bars and lounges and place in safe.
13. Check all cash floats, lock safe and all cupboards.
14. Leave messages for night and morning shift.

These duties are discussed fully in detail in the following chapters.

3.13 RECORDS

Alphabetical guest list (Fig. 3.32)

In large hotels it would be impossible for staff to memorise all the names of the guests and their room numbers. To help facilitate the distribution of mail and delivery of messages an alphabetical guest list is maintained, usually on a revolving stand located in an area easily accessible to all staff of the reception area. These stands can hold several hundred strips, on which are typed the guest's name, initials, room number. Strips are inserted in strict alphabetical order and colours are sometimes used to indicate the type of room, i.e. standard, superior, deluxe or suite.

Name	Initial	Origin	Room number
ACRE	Mr. L	LONDON	307
ADAMS	Mr. B	LEEDS	105
ADAMS	Mr /Mrs C	BRADFORD	209
BROWN	Mrs. J	LONDON	401
COOK	Mrs. L.	LONDON	106
DALY	Mrs. A.	LONDON	409
DEAN	Mr./Mrs.B.J.	LONDON	304
ESSEX	Mr/Mrs/Miss R4	LONDON	402/405
EVANS	Mrs A.J.	BRISTOL	406
FIELD	Mr./Mrs. E	BRISTOL	404
GRIEG	Mr./Mrs. Y.L.	BR OL	410

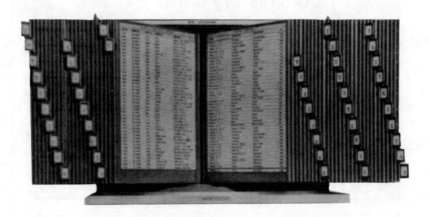

Figure 3.32 *Alphabetical guest list (Roneo Alcatel Ltd)*

Writing of names

A standard method of writing names should be adopted. The surname should be written or typed in block letters followed by the title of the guest, and then the initials. For example:

BARTON MRS/MRS R J·& B L
CARSON MRS/MISS P & J J
JOHNSON CAPT/MRS R S & V
MCALLISTER SIR ROBERT   } Mc, Mac are all treated as Mac; the next letter
MACDONALD MESSRS K & J   } in the name determines the position.
SAINT MR/MRS M & G
ST CLAIRE-LEGGE MR B
STANDISH REV S
WILLIAMS MR/MASTER T & T L

Room history record (Fig. 3.33)

Most hotels maintain records of the occupancy of the room so that at any time they can refer to it and see when and by whom the room was occupied. The room history cards are filed in room number order and must be kept up to date at all times as constant reference is made to them. For example, if any property has been lost or found in the rooms then by referring to the room history card it is possible to discover who was the occupant of the room at a certain date.

Room history card

Room number	Rate		Type
Name	Arrival	Departure	Remarks

Figure 3.33 *Room history card*

Room inventory cards (Fig. 3.34)

These cards are sometimes prepared back-to-back with the room history card (Fig. 3.33) and filed in room order number. They provide details of the furnishings and fittings of each particular type of room. Any repairs or replacements or renewals of furnishings are noted on the cards, and they are constantly referred to by the housekeeping and maintenance departments, whose responsibility it is to see that the room is maintained to the required standard. They provide information for the receptionist when dealing with enquiries for the guests as to what standard equipment is in the room. They are also used by the housekeeper to check that no contents have gone astray.

Room inventory card

Room number 402	Type TWIN BEDDED WITH BATH		Rate £54·00
Fixtures and fittings	Date	Repairs	Renewals
2 SINGLE BEDS			
2 ARMCHAIRS			
2 WARDROBES			
2 BED TABLES			
2 WALL MIRRORS			
1 TELEPHONE			
1 W/PAPER BASKET			
1 ASHTRAY			
2 LUGGAGE RACKS			
1 SQUARE CARPET			

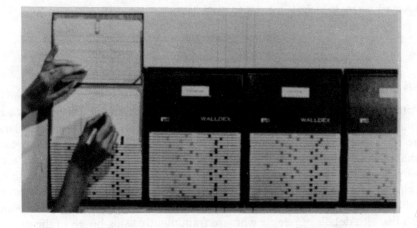

Figure 3.34   *Room inventory cards (Roneo Alcatel Ltd)*

Guest history card (Fig. 3.35)

Some hotels maintain guest history cards. They show the names, addresses, dates of visits to the hotel room occupied, rates, credit ratings, and patronage, and any special likes and dislikes of the guests. These cards are filed in alphabetical order and if used intelligently by the management will provide useful information as to the type of accommodation and service to offer the guest and how to cater for their preferences, and thus promote good public relations. These cards are also useful when doing market research.

Name	Mr. J. Smith			Nationality	British	
Address	16, THE GROVE, ANYTOWN, WESSEX					
Room No.	Date of arrival	Date of departure	Room rate	Total bill	Paid by	Remarks
206	29.3.19 –	7.4.19 –	£25.RB	£157.20	Access	REFER TO MANAGER Habitually drunk, Causing offence to other guests'.

■ A black sticker to indicate a guest on black list

Fig. 3.35   *Guest history card*

Black lists

Some visitors may have proved to be undesirable or objectionable, or perhaps have left without paying their bill, and therefore it is essential that this type of guest be blacklisted for future reference. Sometimes a separate list is prepared but as guest history cards are filed alphabetically coloured stickers can be used, e.g. black which would indicate that a particular person was on the blacklist. Notations are made on the card as to the reasons for blacklisting, and any instructions such as 'refer to manager', 'do not accept' or 'undesirable' should be carefully adhered to by the staff. Sometimes the police will circulate a list with details of people who are fraudulently using hotels in the area. These lists must be carefully noted by the staff.

Reference books

An efficiently organised reception office should always have an up-to-date set of reference books in order to be able to answer the innumerable and varied questions that could be put to them by the guests. The reference library should contain:

1. A Concise Oxford Dictionary.
2. Foreign dictionaries with conversational phrases.
3. *Post Office Guide.*
4. Postal addresses and index to post code directories.
5. Telephone directories — alphabetical and classified.
6. *Telephone Dialling Codes* — an essential booklet providing STD (subscriber trunk dialling) codes.
7. UK Telex directory.
8. *Whitaker's almanack* — a useful source of names and addresses of associations and societies, government offices and national institutions.
9. Kelly's Post Office — London. This publication has a street directory for commercial concerns and information on official, legal, ecclesiastical and local government offices and personnel in the area.
10. Information and guide books on London and other places of geographical and historical interest in Great Britain.
11. A London Underground route map.
12. *Fodor's Guide to Europe* (for overseas visitors).
13. *Bartholomews Gazeteer.* This gives names of cities, towns, villages, rivers, lakes etc. in the British Isles with details of situations, populations and, in the case of large towns or cities, of government buildings.
14. Timetables of local bus services.
15. British Rail timetables.
16. Rail guide.
17. Cooks' continental timetable.
18. World airways guide.
19. Air/rail guide Europe.
20. *National Express Guide to Express Services* — a guide to coach travel within Great Britain.
21. AA and RAC guide books.
22. Maps of the locality.
23. A local guide book.
24. A local paper.
25. A current entertainments page from the local press.
26. Local trade associations' and professional bodies' directories.
27. Local physicians list in case a doctor is required.
28. *Crockfords' Clerical Directory* (C of E clergy).
29. *Who's Who* — names of distinguished people.
30. *Burke's Peerage* — useful for all questions on social precedence.
31. *Black's Titles and Forms of address* — how to address titled people.

3.14 COMMUNICATIONS

PBX (private branch exchange)
The telephone service in most establishments involves the use of a private branch exchange. The PBX is a switchboard connected to a public exchange by one or more lines, and extension telephones in the various offices and departments. Calls must pass through the switchboard with the minimum delay and maximum courtesy. Even the most efficient switchboard operator will at times dial a wrong number or make an incorrect connection, but this should never cause impatience or anger, the error should be corrected as quickly as possible in a pleasing and charming manner.

PABX (private automatic branch exchange) (Fig. 3.36)
This system combines exchange services with automatic intercommunication facilities. Each telephone instrument had its own dial and from it can be dialled other extensions as well as outside calls.

   The operator is only used to give special service to customers and to connect incoming calls, while the extensions have the convenience and speed of dialling their own calls.

Figure 3.36   *PABX*

PBMX (private manual branch exchange) (Fig. 3.37)
This system requires an operator and the board can be switch or cord operated. The operator makes all the incoming, outgoing and internal connections.

Push-button intercom system
This telephone system provides communication between each extension as well as connections to the public exchange.

Loudspeaking device
This is attached to the telephone to enable several people to listen to a call simultaneously and it is also useful if you wish to keep your hands free during a call.

Figure 3.37 *PMBX*

Automatic answering telephone
A device can be fitted to the telephone which enables callers to hear a prerecorded announcement and dictate a message onto a tape. This is extremely useful if the office has to be left unattended for any period of time.

Executive bleeps
This is an electronic system whereby executives are issued with small bleepers. If they are urgently required their 'executive number' is tapped and an electronic signal is sent out which activates their particular 'bleep'. They will then go to the nearest telephone and receive their message from the operator.

Freefone
The establishment undertakes to pay in advance for incoming calls. The caller dials the freefone number and is connected by the operator on a transfer charge basis.

ADC (advice of duration and charge)
The cost of a call made by an operator will be notified to the caller on its completion.

Transfer charge calls (collect calls)
The charge for the call can be transferred to the number called if it is accepted when the operator offers the call.

Fixed time calls
A call can be booked in advance with the operator to be connected at a specified time.

STD (subscriber trunk dialling)
The subscriber can dial trunk calls direct by prefixing the STD number to the number they wish to call. Booklets are provided by Telecom giving lists of STD area code numbers, e.g. 0273 (area) 21345 (subscriber's number).

IDD (international direct dialling)
It is now possible to dial direct to many countries throughout the world. The IDD
number prefixes the number to be called, e.g. 0101 (America) 813 (Florida) 377 (area)
4307 (subscriber's number).

Modern communication systems

The reception office has the responsibility of maintaining the communication services
between the guest and the hotel and internally between the departments within the hotel.
Modern microprocessors and computer technology have made such rapid advances that
telecommunications and internal communications systems are now in compact units
without plugs, switches, or buttons: just small keyboards with touch-sensitive depres-
sions, some with small visual display units (VDUs) which can show at a glance the status
of all calls being handled and prompt the operator through every procedure so that
training can be reduced to a minimum.
    Some modern telephone communication systems have as many as 26 exchange lines
and 134 extensions providing the following:

Facilities
1.   All others extensions can be dialled from the front office. If an extension is engaged
     or does not reply, a simple code can be dialled which monitors the extension you
     require. When it is free the system will automatically connect to the extension user
     who gave the code.
2.   When dealing with an enquiry, the call can be held whilst the enquiry is being made.
3.   A call can be transferred to another extension.
4.   A conference system can be set up whereby up to six people can listen and talk
simultaneously.
5.   Calls can be diverted to other extensions if the office is very busy or unstaffed.

Special features for hotels

Electronic room status boards.	The status of every room can be displayed, enabling the reception office to tell at a glance whether a room is occupied, waiting to be cleaned or ready for the next guest.
Wake up calls.	Guests can program their own wake up calls on the telephone.
Message waiting.	The switchboard can automatically call the guest's room at regular intervals until a reply is received.
Call metering.	Guests can make their own private calls and the metered units will be recorded automatically against their room. Details can be recorded on an electronic printer.
Room monitors.	Reception can monitor a room where a child has been left.
Priority calling.	Preferential telephone service can be given to VIP guests.
Rooms service.	Guests can call a range of services from their own rooms by dialling or keying one digit.
Do not disturb.	This is a service whereby all calls can be routed to the operator.
Call barring.	This is an unobtrusive way of keeping expensive unofficial calls to the minimum. The system can be instructed to prevent individual extensions from making certain calls such as IDD (international direct dialling) and STD (subscriber trunk dialling).

Figure 3.38 *Monarch system*

Figure 3.39   *Teleprinter*

Telex and teleprinter (Fig. 3.39)

A teleprinter is a machine with a typewriter keyboard on which messages can be typed and reproduced on a teleprinter at the end of the wire.

Modern technology is now so sophisticated the microprocessor-based design of the teleprinter gives it enormous power and flexibility.

Some features of the modern teleprinter
1. Alphanumerical keys are arranged like a conventional typewriter.
2. There are integrated visual display units attached.
3. Telex messages can be typed direct into the teleprinter's memory and automatically transmitted at a preset time.
4. Messages can be received and transmitted automatically whilst the operator is preparing another message on the screen.
5. Incoming messages can be stored in the teleprinter's memory until the printer is free, or by pressing an attend call an incoming message can be given priority.
6. The same message can be transmitted to several different destinations.
7. The contents of any message stored in the teleprinter's memory can be viewed on the visual display unit.
8. Word-processing facilities can be incorporated, giving fast and efficient message editing. Letters, words or whole lines can be deleted and new texts inserted at the touch of a button.

Prestel (Figs. 3.40, 3.41)

Prestel is a new kind of information service used by customers in Britain and overseas. An adapted television set and an ordinary telephone line link the prestel customer to an enormous range of computer-held information. By pressing numbered buttons on a small key pad a page of information appears on the television screen.

British Telecom have launched 'Room Service', which is an electronic booking system linking all Prestel users with more than 1000 hotels throughout the world. It lists rooms and amenities available at each hotel. To use 'Room Service' customers specify the area in which they intend to stay. An index showing hotels and rates in that area appears on the screen. Having decided on the hotel the customer is then able to fill in the requirement on a booking page which is then transmitted to the hotel.

Figure 3.40 *Prestel*

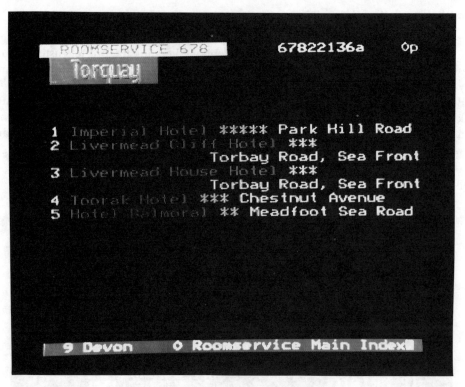

Figure 3.41 *Prestel*

Hotel Television Network (HTN)

This service funded by National Advertisers is an addition to the normal TV channels. It is a free television channel to three- to five-star hotels in London. Programmes include a London guide to shopping, entertainment, theatre and Cinema reviews, tourist attractions, news of forthcoming events, feature films, guide book information, leaflets and maps and teletext information.

3.15 PROGRESS TEST QUESTIONS

1. Define the following terms:
    (a) en pension;
    (b) demi-pension;
    (c) rack rate;
    (d) American plan;
    (e) modified American plan;
    (f) European plan;
    (g) shoulder period.
2. Define the following terms:
    (a) VIPs and CIPs;

    (b)   back-to-back reservations;

    (c)   A & TO;

    (d)   T or P;

    (e)   no show;

    (f)   6 p.m. release;

    (g)   guaranteed arrival;

    (h)   hotel discount card.

3. Define the use and purpose of the following, using diagrams to illustrate your answers when necessary:

    (a)   the conventional reservation chart;

    (b)   a reception board;

    (c)   the hotel diary;

    (d)   the arrivals and departures list;

    (e)   the alphabetical guest list.

4. Explain how the hotel could check the credit-worthiness of a guest.

5. The hotel receives a letter from Mr and Mrs Jones who wish to reserve a double room with bath from 7–14 June. Explain briefly how you would deal with the request and then process the reservation from the arrival to the final departure of the guests.

6. Explain briefly how:

    (a)   the Whitney reservations system operates;

    (b)   an electronic room status board operates.

7. Explain how an 'electronic key system' operates and its advantages.

8. The Silver Star tour operator wishes to book accommodation with the Royal Hotel for a group of 20 people on a package tour. Detail briefly the step-by-step procedure of handling the booking from the time the enquiry is made to the departure of the guests.

9. How does the central reservations system operate?

10. A guest wishes to change rooms. What action would you take to ensure all records are amended and all departments are notified?

11. A guest requests that you accept a jewel box and a bundle of notes for safe-keeping. Describe the procedures in this instance, illustrating your answer with diagrams of the records that should be kept.

12. A group of five guests are due to arrive at 9.30 p.m. What action should be taken and what instructions would be left with the evening shift?

13. You are a head receptionist at a medium-sized hotel, instructing a new trainee receptionist. Write briefly on how you would explain some of the tasks that have to be carried out:

    (a)   on the morning shift 8 a.m.–3 p.m.

    (b)   on the evening shift 3 p.m.–11 p.m.

14. Detail some of the features of modern hotel communication systems.

15. Explain briefly the following terms:

    (a)   PBX;

    (b)   PABX;

    (c)   PMBX;

    (d)   executive 'bleeps';

    (e)   Freefone;

    (f)   ADC;

    (g)   STD;

    (h)   IDD;

    (i)   telex.

16.   What 'books of reference' would you use to deal with the following enquiries:

    (a)   the address of the nearest dentist;

    (b)   train or bus service;

    (c)   places of historical interest in the locality;

    (d)   what is on at the local theatre;

    (e)   postal charges to Japan;

    (f)   the distance by road between two points;

    (g)   the address of the local chamber of commerce?

4 Selling and marketing

4.1 SELLING TECHNIQUES FOR THE RECEPTIONIST

Successful selling not only maximises the profitability of the hotel but, more to the point, assists customer satisfaction by offering food, accommodation and services at a price the guest can afford.

In order to sell accommodation successfully receptionists must learn how to use their eyes, ears and intelligence in order to assess their clients and their needs. All guests will differ emotionally, physically and temperamentally and will have a wide variety of likes, dislikes, tastes and income levels.

The receptionist must have a complete knowledge of the hotel, the rooms, types, location, furnishings and rates, and all the other facilities the hotel has to offer.

As the management will be aiming for maximum room and bed occupancy practice and experience will train the receptionist how to plan bookings on the conventional chart (Fig. 3.11) so that one letting follows another and no gaps are left unnecessarily.

Simple rules to be followed when selling accommodation

1. Whenever possible, rooms are let floor by floor upwards, grouped together. This helps facilitate the organisation of labour and the servicing of rooms.
2. Select rooms to be offered which are within the apparent price range appropriate to the guest.
3. Do not confuse the guest by offering too wide a variety of rooms. Confine the selection to one or two at a time.
4. Always tactfully ascertain whether a couple would prefer a double-bedded room or a twin-bedded room.
5. Families may require adjoining or adjacent rooms.
6. Bear in mind that elderly, handicapped or disabled people will not want stairs to climb or long walks to lifts, stairs, public rooms or restaurants.
7. Before offering accommodation try to ascertain any preference the guest may have, such as for a room with a view or a room away from traffic and noise.
8. If a person requests a single room and none is available, offer a twin-bedded room as opposed to a double as it is more economical to change a single bed than a double. When all single rooms have been sold hotels may offer their twin-bedded rooms or double rooms at a reduced rate. This is known as 'middle rate' for single occupancy.
9. The management will obviously expect their reception staff to sell the higher priced accommodation whenever possible, but it must be borne in mind that the interests of the client must come first, for a happy satisfied guest will return and spread goodwill.

4.2 RECEPTION AS A SALES DEPARTMENT

In any organisation people are either the strongest or weakest link, and all operations within that business will depend on their ability to listen, think, remember, communicate and act, and the impact of their performance, either on the technical side or on the side dealing with the public, will invariably have a profound effect on the selling of their product which, in the hotel industry, is accommodation, food, drink and hospitality. There is no substitute for knowledge and above all the reception staff must have a complete knowledge of the product they are selling if they are going to sell effectively.

The receptionist must be thoroughly familiar with the following:

(a) all of the information contained in the hotel brochure;
(b) details of tariff changes, special rates, and discounts, charges for children, pets, etc.;
(c) all the general facts and figures appertaining to the size, shape and types of rooms, their fixtures and furnishings; any special information relating to the lounges, bars and restaurants, swimming pool, sports facilities, hairdressing, valeting, shops theatre tickets, etc.
(d) information on transport connections to and from the hotel by road, rail, sea and air and car hire;
(e) parking facilities at and available to the hotel;
(f) details of facilities and equipment available in the hotel for conferences, special functions and other events;
(g) details of all types of menu offered by the hotel and times of service;
(h) information on facilities for the elderly, handicapped, children and pets;
(i) information on special offers for mid-week and weekend breaks, package holidays, Easter and Christmas special programmes;
(j) the entertainment programmes offered by the hotel;
(k) information on local events, entertainments and places of interest in the area;
(l) details of travel agents, tour operators, airlines, business organisations, and central reservations numbers with whom contact can be made if accommodation becomes available;
(m) rules and regulations relating to arrival and check out times, methods of payment accepted, chance business, licensing for special functions etc.;
(n) any other specialised information regarding the hotel.

To develop their awareness and need to know their product simple questionnaires could be put to the staff along the lines of:

1. Describe the layout of the room in the hotel used for functions.
2. Describe the layout of a room for a conference of fifteen.
3. Give details of the luncheon table d'hote menu.
4. Give details of the entertainment provided by the hotel for a mini break.
5. For a special function, how would one obtain an extended licence?
6. What are the maximum covers the hotel can take for a banquet?
7. Does the hotel provide a playroom for children? If so, describe a range of toys for ages up to twelve.
8. What hours does the swimming instructor attend the pool?

4.3 METHODS OF SELLING

By letter
Any enquiries by letter should be dealt with immediately by return enclosing the hotel brochure, tariff and any other relevant information that will assist the sale.

By telephone
A good telephone voice is a considerable asset as its tone and manner will create an impression in the minds of the enquirer. When dealing with a telephone enquiry it is essential that all the necessary information is at the fingertips of the receptionist as nothing is more irritating on the telephone than hesitancy through lack of knowledge or being asked to hang on whilst information is being looked up — and always have alternatives to offer if the first choice is not available.

Personal selling
Whether by telephone or face-to-face, personal selling is an art, and a good selling technique can be developed so that with quiet confidence, knowledge and enthusiasm for the product the receptionist can highlight the special features of the establishment, so that in the minds of the customer that particular establishment has something extra special to offer. For example, instead of just stating the facts about the accommodation and facilities of the hotel one could add small descriptive notes without exaggerating. For example:

Question   Is the hotel central?
Answer   Yes — we are very centrally situated for all forms of entertainment, theatres, parks and public transport.

Question   Are there any parking facilities?
Answer   Yes, we are fortunate; we have uncovered parking, and there are ample other parking facilities nearby.

Question   What facilities are there in the rooms?
Answer   Every room has a nineteen inch colour television, tea-making facilities and a direct dialling telephone system.

Question   Is there an extra charge for a child of nine?
Answer   No, there is no extra charge for children under twelve, and we have a small playroom for young children in the hotel.

Question   Is there a night service?
Answer   We have a night service porter on duty and he will be pleased to provide late snacks if required.

The list is endless and a good receptionist will seize every opportunity to sell the services of the hotel without over-selling and appearing pushy, so that the highly developed selling technique becomes an art.

4.4 SELLING TO THE BUSINESS PERSON

By land, sea and air, international travel is now fast, easy and quite commonplace. A great deal of hotel business comes from people travelling not just for holidays or sightseeing but by people travelling by virtue of their business activities. When selling services to the business person one must remember that the circumstances and their needs will differ:

1. Business people are usually travelling at the company's expense and are unlikely to be on a strict budget. They will probably require room service and avail themselves of the amenities of the hotel.
2. They are travelling out of necessity not for pleasure, therefore, the hotel must be a home from home, and they will most likely eat and drink in the hotel.
3. Time will probably be of the essence; therefore, they will want a quick efficient service of check in and check out, and possibly room service or late night snacks.
4. They may require a television and radio in the room and a flat surface on which to work at their business papers. They may also require secretarial services if available at the hotel, and a direct dialling telephone.
5. If the services are satisfactory the business people are quite likely to become regular visitors and recommend the hotel to their business associates.
6. There are no high or low seasons for business people and they will often require their accommodation at short notice. Many large business houses have a regular room allocation with hotels which can be placed on release after a certain time lapse if not required. Some hotels maintain ledger accounts for the regular business users and the account is sent direct to the companies which enables a speedy departure for the guest.

4.5 CONFERENCE AND BANQUETING BUSINESS

Trade exhibitions, seminars, workshops, conventions and conferences, have now become a specialised market and it has been quoted, even at a conservative estimate, that there is at least ten million pounds worth of business available through conference agencies.

It is an increasingly competitive market and conference organisers whose function it is to provide complete package deals for buyers are continually looking for new hotels and venues that can provide something different every year.

It is not only the very large hotels which enter into this market: smaller hotels with twenty bedrooms upwards, a quiet fair-sized conference room, good bedrooms and adequate facilities can compete for the smaller trade exhibitions, training courses, seminars and conferences.

Hotels with only the basic facilities can attract this type of business by putting together composite package deals and offering them to the conference agencies. To this end managers should follow:

1. Study what has been successful and popular in the past.
2. Consider the size, structure and special features of the hotel and what special type of event it could lend itself to, e.g. mediaeval banquets etc.
3. Study the locality and its geographical, historical or sporting interests, e.g. stately homes, good golf courses, marinas, etc.

4. Structure a conference social programme, including sporting programmes, evening entertainments, and ladies' programmes, for delegates' wives and husbands.
5. To be successful the hotel will provide a friendly atmosphere, good service and the personal touch. They will ascertain the conference buyer's need and structure their services to meet these needs.

Large conferences

The very large hotels are comfortably geared to provide the venue for any type of conference, large or small. They usually have a wide range of rooms available with major conference and banqueting areas supplemented by smaller syndicate rooms, private suites and other facilities.

Hotels offering these types of facilities usually have their own carefully prepared brochures, describing the area and giving full details as follows:

Dimensions of rooms
(a) floor area;
(b) room length;
(c) room width;
(d) ceiling heights.

Maximum capacity each room will take for:
(a) lunch/dinner — round tables, sprigs;
(b) dinner dance;
(c) cocktail reception;
(d) fashion show;
(e) stage show;
(f) conference only: school room style, cinema style;
(g) conference with lunch/dinner.

Other information on:
(a) air conditioning;
(b) sound insulation;
(c) lighting equipment;
(d) technological equipment AV/Film/VTR;
(e) access for loading and unloading equipment;
(f) space for exhibition booths;
(g) telephone points;
(h) switches;
(i) power socket outlets;
(j) TV outlets (closed circuits etc.).
(k) microphone sockets;
(l) audio jack outlets;
(m) amplifiers;
(n) moveable partitions, blackboards, flipboards;
(o) clocks;
(p) direct dialling services;
(q) emergency exits.

Secretarial services:
(a) telex;
(b) photocopying;
(c) printing of schedules, lists, speeches, name tags, menus, give aways;
(d) translation service.

Colourful pictorial brochures are circulated to all conference agencies and enquirers can then contact and discuss package deals with the hotels offering the services.

Conference booking

When a conference is booked the management will discuss full details and prepare a check list with the organisers, detailing all their requirements. When this is finalised and agreed, schedules will be prepared and put into action.

1. Rooms will be booked for VIPs, delegates and their spouses (if applicable) and organisers.
2. Meeting rooms and equipment required will be booked, planned and organised.
3. Food and beverage departments will be given a detailed schedule of meals required.
4. All departments involved will be notified and given detailed schedules.
5. Any other action necessary will be taken.

   The success of this type of operation depends on planning, organisation, attention to detail, efficiency of staff and complete co-operation from all departments.
   If a hotel gains a reputation for high standards and professionalism in handling this type of business, that will be a recommendation in itself.

4.6 MARKETING

The term 'marketing' started gaining prominence in the business arena after the Second World War. Today the marketing executive has the responsibility for co-ordinating all aspects of a product or service: packaging, labelling and presenting the product in a manner likely to improve its saleability, then fully exploiting existing markets, always thinking of new ideas and plans for creating new markets. Marketing a 'product' like the hotels, catering, hospitality and tourism industry involves several factors, as follows.

Market research and analysis (Fig. 4.1)
Continual research into market trends provided by the statistics and information contained in sales analysis, guest record cards, guest history cards and trade magazines. Questionnaires in the rooms inviting the guests to comment on the standards of facilities and service and what extra facilities the guests would like incorporated is another method of providing ideas on how to improve the saleability of the product.

Promotional literature
Brochures and tariffs should be well designed, colourful and descriptive. If the Hotel is part of a group, brochures of other hotels within the group should be on display and receptionists instructed to see that they are well distributed to guests and casual enquirers.

GRAND HOTEL
****

To assist us in maintaining our high standards may we solicit your comments on our performance?

Thank you.

Please tick ✓

	Excellent	Good	Satisfactory	Unsatisfactory
1 How was your reservation handled? By direct reservation By central reservations				
2 How do you rate the following: Reception desk service Porter/bellman service Telephone service TV reception Room cleanliness Room charges				
3 How do your rate our food service: Quality of food Quality of service Menu selection Prices Cleanliness				
4 How do your rate our cocktail lounge: Quality of beverages Quality of service Prices Entertainment				
5 How do you rate the hotel facilities				

6 What do you like most about our hotel ....

7 What do you like least about our hotel ....
....

8 Personal comments ....
....
....
....

Date   Room No.   Name and address if you wish

We thank you for staying with us and appreciate your comments. Please be assured they will be given every consideration — after all we hope to you again!
From the entire Grand Hotel staff.

Figure 4.1 *Typical market research questionnaire*

Promotional 'give-aways'
Give-away packs in guest rooms are designed to create a welcoming impression in the guest's mind, whilst promoting the name and the facilities offered by the hotel. Give-aways such as book matches, note pads, pens, pencils, diaries, calendars and stationery, can be regarded as a good investment if they promote the good image of the establishment.

Personal selling
All members of staff, in particular the reception and contact staff, must be trained in the development of selling techniques and good public relations. They must know their product thoroughly and how to promote sales by word of mouth, telephone or correspondence. Staff should be involved in the marketing and sales programmes and targets should be set and staff rewarded if they are achieved.

Advertising
The method of advertising used will depend largely on the 'advertising or marketing budget', but the product can be advertised using several different types of media and the hotel or hotel group will select the method that will give them the best coverage within their financial means.
   Types of advertising include:

(a)   the press — national and local newspapers, trade magazines, guide books, local magazines;
(b)   posters at air terminals, railway stations, buses, hoardings;
(c)   radio;
(d)   television;
(e)   direct mail;
(f)   newsletters.

Travel agents and tour operators' promotions
Package deals promoted by travel agents and tour operators are increasingly being used to promote sales during off-season periods. Colourful brochures and posters proclaim bargain weekends, mini breaks, etc. The promoters are also marketing imaginative packages which sometimes include books of vouchers giving entrance to places of historical or geographical interest, discounted theatre tickets, unlimited travel on the bus or underground, tee shirts and other promotional give-aways as well as hotel accommodation and meals.

Promoting special services and events
Many hotels are showing enterprise and imagination by staging special events, such as golfing weekends and gourmet holidays where the emphasis is on specially prepared gourmet meals, trekking holidays, tudor banquets, etc. These types of events are well advertised in the appropriate magazines, and the hotels gain a reputation for this type of promotion which appeals to people who are looking for a change or something different.

Promoting family weekend breaks
The weekend break has now become a regular feature amongst the many special offers by hotels. Attractive brochures illustrating all the additional facilities of the hotel, such as coffee bars, discos, saunas, swimming pools, tennis courts, golf courses, bars and

restaurants are aimed at attracting the family. Large bedrooms with two large beds accommodating the family for little or no extra cost means revenue from extra meals and drinks. Weekend hostesses organise special tours and entertainments, welcome drinks, tee shirts and children's entertainment, and special vouchers give cheap entrance to local attractions such as safari parks or stately homes. Ingredients like these add to the promotion of this type of package deal.

Many London hotels offer a similar weekend break at special prices encouraging people to take in the sights and pageantry of the capital city. This type of package is sometimes offered in conjunction with cheap rail fares and bus vouchers.

Overseas marketing

A report by the British Tourist Authority estimated that twelve million overseas visitors came to the United Kingdom in 1982, spending in the region of two thousand million pounds. In July and August approximately two million visitors came to London attracted by the historical interest and other events and places common only to the British Isles. Typical package tours marketed abroad are 'the grand tour of historical Britain', Wimbledon, and the British Open Golf Championships, stately homes of England, the castles of Scotland. The tours usually includes air travel accommodation and organised escorted tours.

4.7 PROGRESS TEST QUESTIONS

1. What are the basic rules to be followed when selling accommodation from the reception desk?
2. Discuss the statement 'there is no substitute for product knowledge', relating it to the receptionist as a salesperson.
3. Give five illustrations of using good sales technique.
4. How does the method of selling to a business person and a tourist differ?
5. What essential information would need to be available when dealing with an enquiry from a conference organiser?
6. Define the term 'marketing'.
7. Suggest the methods you would use to promote:
   (a) a weekend break in a country hotel;
   (b) a weekend break at a London hotel;
   (c) a tour of the Scottish highlands.

5 Book-keeping*

5.1 BASIC PRINCIPLES OF DOUBLE-ENTRY BOOK-KEEPING

Book-keeping is the recording of the transactions of a business in a simple and reliable manner in order to provide the trader with information to show:

(a) the trader's financial position;
(b) whether the business is making a profit or loss and how this profit or loss is made up.

Double entry

The double-entry system is the basis of modern systems used by businesses both large and small, governments, banks, insurance companies and industries. It records the two-fold effect of every business transaction. For instance, if a business sells ten pounds worth of goods for cash, the goods go out of the business as sales and the cash comes into the business. If goods are sold and payment postponed until a later date, we still have ten pounds of value in goods going out of the business, and we have a debtor who represents ten pounds worth of debt owing to us. Every business transaction will therefore require two entries to be made in our books — one representing *value going out*, the other representing *value coming in*. In order to record this we must divide our accounts into two sides. The left hand side is known as the *debit* (entry for value coming in) and the right hand side the *credit* (entry for value going out). Therefore, every time an entry is made on the debit side, another entry of equal value must be made on the credit side somewhere in the books.

Every debit must have a corresponding credit and vice-versa. The whole of the double-entry system is based upon this principle and it follows from this principle that at any time the total debits must equal the total credits and by adding the two a check can be made on the double entry; this is one of the main advantages of the system.

The ledger

The core of the double-entry system is the ledger, in which all the transactions of the business must ultimately appear, either individually or as totals from subsidiary books, as shown by Fig. 5.1. The ledger is a book of accounts.

---

* For a more detailed coverage of this subject see the authors' *Book-keeping and Accounts for Hotel and Catering Studies* (Holt, Rinehart and Winston, 1983).

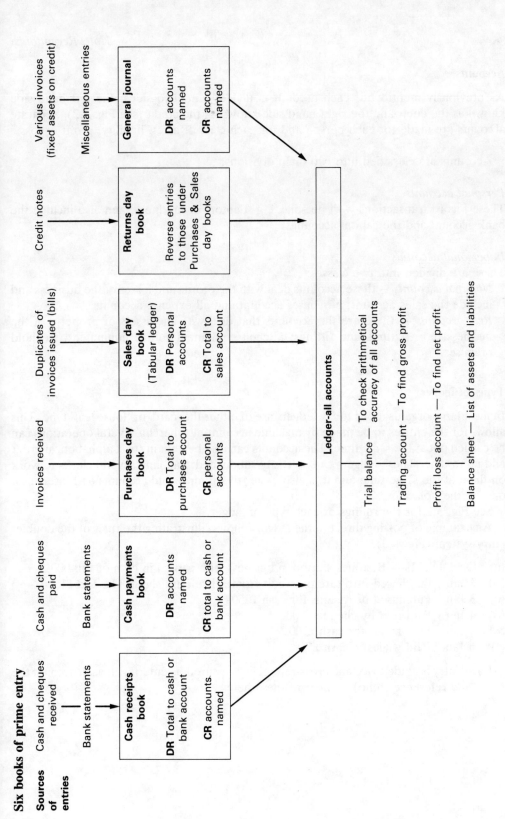

Six books of prime entry

Sources of entries					
Cash and cheques received	Cash and cheques paid	Invoices received	Duplicates of invoices issued (bills)	Credit notes	Various invoices (fixed assets on credit)
Bank statements	Bank statements				Miscellaneous entries

Cash receipts book
DR Total to cash or bank account
CR accounts named

Cash payments book
DR accounts named
CR total to cash or bank account

Purchases day book
DR Total to purchases account
CR personal accounts

Sales day book (Tabular ledger)
DR Personal accounts
CR Total to sales account

Returns day book
Reverse entries to those under Purchases & Sales day books

General journal
DR accounts named
CR accounts named

Ledger-all accounts

Trial balance — To check arithmetical accuracy of all accounts

Trading account — To find gross profit

Profit loss account — To find net profit

Balance sheet — List of assets and liabilities

Figure 5.1 *The double-entry book-keeping system*

Accounts

As previously mentioned, each account is divided into two sides, the left hand side known as the debit and the right hand side known as the credit (see Fig. 5.2). Separate accounts are made for each person and for each class of asset, liability, profit or loss.

Accounts are classified into two main divisions.

Personal accounts
These record transactions with persons, e.g. debtors or creditors, and also include the bank account and the capital account.

Impersonal accounts
These are divided into two classes:
Nominal accounts — these accounts deal with the profits and losses of the business and include the sales account, purchases account and all expense accounts.
Real accounts — these are the accounts that deal with the assets or property of the business, e.g. fixtures and fittings; kitchen equipment; office equipment; freehold premises.

Types of ledger

In most large organisations today ledgers are of either the 'card' or 'loose leaf' type. This allows for the entries to be made by machine accounting whereby several operations can be carried out at the same time. The accounts can also be kept in strict alphabetical order and up to date. These ledgers can be easily subdivided, enabling several clerks to work on them at the same time and it is also easier to withdraw old accounts and insert new ones in their place.

See Fig. 5.2 for the rulings of each type of ledger.

An example of posting direct to the ledger follows, illustrating the rules of the double-entry system (Fig. 5.3):

(a)　On 1 Jan. 19— B. Jones started in business with capital in cash of £10 000.
(b)　2 Jan.　Purchased furniture on credit from Mitre Furnishings Co. Ltd £1500.
(c)　3 Jan.　Purchased provisions for cash £250.
(d)　4 Jan.　Paid rent by cheque £500.
(e)　5 Jan.　Sold meals for cash £200.
(f)　6 Jan.　Paid wages in cash £55.

Each entry is made twice and cross-reference is assured by entering in each account the name and reference (folio) number of the other.

Ledger card   Number _____

Brown Alan W., Water Street, Sutton

Date	Particulars	Folio	Debit	Credit	Balance

Figure 5.2(a)   *Ledger card (mechanised system)*

Ledger book   Number _____

Dr   Cr

Date	Details	Folio	£	P	Date	Details	Folio	£	P

Figure 5.2(b)   *Ledger book (manual system)*

CAPITAL – B. JONES   A/C 1

Date	Details	Folio	£	p	Date	Details	Folio	£	p
19..					19..				
					Jan.1	Cash	2	10,000	00

CASH / BANK   A/C 2

Date	Details	Folio	£	p	Date	Details	Folio	£	p
19..					19..				
Jan.1	Capital – B. Jones	1	10,000	00	Jan.3	Purchases	5	250	00
" 5	Sales	7	200	00	" 4	Rent	6	500	00
					" 6	Wages	8	55	00

FURNITURE   A/C 3

Date	Details	Folio	£	p	Date	Details	Folio	£	p
19..					19..				
Jan.2	Mitre Furnishings Co.Ltd 4		15,00	00					

MITRE FURNISHINGS CO. LTD   A/C 4

Date	Details	Folio	£	p	Date	Details	Folio	£	p
19..					19..				
					Jan.2	Furniture	3	1500	00

PURCHASES   A/C 5

Date	Details	Folio	£	p	Date	Details	Folio	£	p
19..					19..				
Jan.3	Cash	2	250	00					

RENT   A/C 6

Date	Details	Folio	£	p	Date	Details	Folio	£	p
19..					19..				
Jan.4	Cash	2	500	00					

SALES   A/C 7

Date	Details	Folio	£	p	Date	Details	Folio	£	p
19..					19..				
					Jan.5	Cash	2	200	00

WAGES   A/C 8

Date	Details	Folio	£	p	Date	Details	Folio	£	p
19..					19..				
Jan.6	Cash	2	55	00					

Figure 5.3   *Illustration of posting direct to the ledger*

Examples of posting to an account

Example 1

On 1 March 19— A. Debtor, who has an account with the Atlas Hotel, owed the hotel £23.50. On 7 March he entertained at the hotel — the bill No. 216 amounting to £16.50 was posted to his account. On 8 March an allowance due to an overcharge on wine was posted to A. Debtor's account. On 31 March a cheque was received from A. Debtor in settlement of his account less an agreed discount of five per cent.

Solution

Dr.				A. Debtor				Cr.
19 . .			£	19 . .				£
Mar. 1	Balance	b/d	23.50	Mar. 8	Allowance			2.00
Mar. 7	Bill 216		16.50	Mar. 31	Cheque			36.10
					Discount			1.90
			£40.00					£40.00

Example 2

On 1 September 19— A. Creditor, who is a supplier to the Atlas Hotel, was owed by the hotel the amount of £85.00. On 3 September he supplied goods to the hotel valued £35.00. On 5 September a credit note No. 19 was received from A. Creditor in respect of damaged goods valued £5.00 returned by the hotel. On 30 September the hotel sent A. Creditor a cheque in settlement of the amount owing on 5 September less the agreed five per cent cash discount.

Solution

Dr.			A. Creditor				Cr.
19 . .			£	19 . .			£
Sept. 5	C.N. 19		5.00	Sept. 1	Balance	b/d	85.00
Sept. 30	Cheque		109.25	Sept. 3	Goods		35.00
	Discount		5.75				
			£120.00				£120.00

5.2   BUSINESS DOCUMENTS (SOURCES OF ENTRY — SEE FIG. 5.1)

Order form

Figure 5.6(a)   *Order form*

Whenever a purchase is made an order (using an official order form) should be sent to the supplier. Orders should be in duplicate and numbered and should state exactly the goods required, quoting catalogue numbers when possible. Orders should always be signed by a responsible official.

Delivery note (Fig. 5.6(b))

When goods are delivered they are usually accompanied by a delivery note showing details of items supplied. This delivery note should be used for checking purposes against the goods, and any damage or shortages should be noted.

Invoice (Fig. 5.6(c))

An invoice is a detailed account of goods purchased. It is numbered and shows quantities, quality, prices, packing charges and details of terms and discounts. It is sent by the seller to the customer. Invoices received should be checked for prices and calculations and passed if correct for entry into the appropriate columns of the purchases day book.

Delivery note ABC Suppliers Ltd.
Lonsdale Road,
London S.W.2.
Telephone 01-692 6744

Number ___673___

To QUEEN'S HOTEL
GRAND PARADE
BRASEBOURNE, SUSSEX

Please receive: PER VAN   Date 15th JUNE 19

Order number	Quantity	Pack size	Item		
G 16723	1	10kg	BULK FLOUR		
	1	10kg	SUGAR		
	3	5kg	ICING SUGAR		

1 bag 5 kg icing sugar damaged and returned

Received in good order and condition   Signature A. J. White

Figure 5.6(b) *Delivery note*

Invoice A.B.C. Suppliers Ltd
Lonsdale Road, London S.W.2.
Telephone 01-692 6744

Number   196761

Date   15th June 19

To: Queen's Hotel,
Grand Parade,
Brasebourne,
Sussex.

Order number		Carriage		Terms:	25% trade discount
G 16723		Paid			5% cash discount — 7 days
					2½% cash discount — 30 days

Catalogue reference	Quantity	Pack size	Item	Unit price	£
P3	1	10 kg	Bulk Flour	32p per kg	3.20
P6	1	10 kg	Sugar	51p per kg	5.10
P7	3	5 kg	Icing Sugar	54p per kg	8.10
					16.40
			Less 25% Trade Discount		4.10
				Net	£12.30

Figure 5.6(c) *Invoice*

| Credit note | A.B.C. Suppliers Ltd
Lonsdale Road, London S.W.2.
Telephone 01-692 6744 | Number | C 62 |

| | | Date | 17th June 19 .. |

To: Queen's Hotel,
     Grand Parade,
     Brasebourne,
     Sussex.

Order number

G 16723

Catalogue reference	Quantity	Pack size	Item	Unit price	£
P7	1	5 kg	Icing Sugar Damaged in transit	54p per kg	2.70
			Less 25% Trade Discount		0.67
				Net	£2.03

Figure 5.6(d)   *Credit note — usually printed and/or typed in red*

Credit note (Fig. 5.6(d))

This document is sent by the seller to the customer when goods have been returned or an overcharge has been made. It is numbered and usually printed in red. It shows the customers that their account has been credited with the amount involved. It is entered in the returns day book.

Debit note

This document is sent by the customer to the seller when goods are returned. It shows that the customer has debited the seller's account with the value of the goods returned.

Statement (Fig. 5.6(e))

This is a summarised account usually sent to the customer at the end of each month. It shows the amount owing at the beginning of the period plus the amounts on invoices issued, and deducting any discounts, returns or cash payments. It shows the balance due and is notice that payment is due.

Petty cash voucher (Fig. 5.6(f))

These are numbered, showing details of cash handed out by petty (minor) cashiers. They must be duly authorised and signed by the person receiving the cash. They are entered in the petty cash book.

Statement

A.B.C. Suppliers Ltd
Lonsdale Road, London S.W.2.
Telephone 01-692 6744

To   Date 30th June 19..

Queen's Hotel,
Grand Parade,
Brasebourne,
Sussex.

Date	Reference	Details		Debit £	Credit £	Balance £
197..						
June 1	—	Balance	b/fwd.			220.00
2	196740	Goods		54.20		274.20
3	196744	Goods		32.10		306.30
4	—	Cash			209.50	86.30
		Discount			10.50	
8	196752	Goods		25.40		111.70
15	196761	Goods		12.30		124.00
17	Cr.N.62	Returns			2.03	121.97
28	196790	Goods		42.43		164.40

Terms:	5% cash discount — 7 days 2½% cash discount — 30 days	Amount due	£ 164.40

Figure 5.6(e)   *Statement of account*

Petty cash voucher

Details	Amount	
ERASERS, BIROS	1	35
Total £	1	35

Date 6 JAN 19—   Signature J. Jones
Voucher number 8   Passed by A J White

Figure 5.6(f)   *Petty cash voucher*

5.3 SUBSIDIARY BOOKS

It would be possible to record every business transaction directly into the ledger, but the volume would be very great; therefore, most businesses keep subsidiary books, or books of prime entry as they are called, and post only the totals periodically to the appropriate account in the ledger. In addition to the basic six books of prime entry a petty cash book is also kept to avoid having to enter petty or small cash payments into the main cash book and this is discussed in more detail later in the chapter (see Fig. 5.6(f)). A separate wages book is also kept.

Purchases day book

Most establishments keep their purchases day book in the form of a weekly invoice summary sheet, which is analysed (see Fig. 5.7). This assists the management in exercising cost control on commodities.

The general journal

The journal is a book of prime entry used to record transactions which do not pass through the cash receipts or payments books, or purchases, sales or returns day books, for example, purchases and sales of fixed assets on credit, the correction of errors and other entries of an extraordinary nature. A journal entry consists of three parts:

(a)   the debit entry (Dr);
(b)   the credit entry (Cr);
(c)   the narration — this is a short note of explanation.

Example:

The Journal

19 . .		Fol.	Debit	Credit
			£	£
June 1	Restaurant Furniture DR		500.00	
	Martin Furniture Co. Ltd.			500.00
	Being the purchase of *new Restaurant*			
	furniture, Invoice 320.			

Figure 5.8

Returns outwards

It frequently occurs that goods have to be returned to suppliers for various reasons, e.g. damaged or defective goods. The suppliers then send the customer a credit note to show that they have credited the customer's account with the amount involved. The credit note is entered in the customer's returns outwards book and in turn posted to the suppliers' ledger accounts. Total returns outwards are deducted from the purchases account.

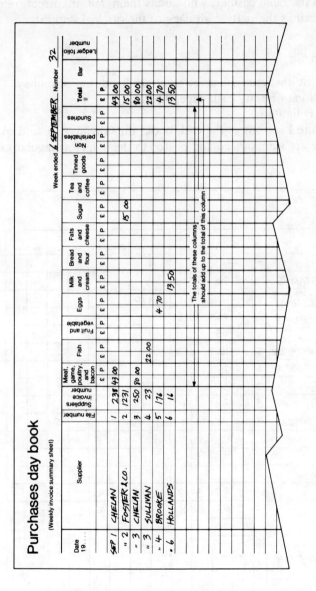

Figure 5.7 *Purchases day book (analysed)*

Petty cash book (see Fig. 5.9)

In most businesses it is usual to keep a petty cash book for the payment of small expenses. This petty cash is kept on the *imprest system*, whereby the petty cashier is entrusted with a fixed sum of money. This is called the imprest, and out of this he or she makes all small payments. Periodically the petty cashier presents the petty cash book, receipts and vouchers to the head cashier, who audits them and, if correct, reimburses the amount spent. This brings the petty cash back to the original imprest.

Advantages of the system

1. The petty cashier must always account for a certain fixed sum of money.
2. There is regular auditing of petty cash expenditure.
3. The chance of theft is limited.
4. Small items of cash are kept out of the cash book, thus saving time and space.
5. Items of expenditure are summarised and posted to the ledger at regular intervals.

Petty cash book

Dr.   Cr.

Imprest	Date	Details	Folio	Total	Postages	Travel expenses	Stationery	Carriage	Visitors paid out	Sundries
15 00	19- JAN 1	IMPREST	–	—						
	" 2	POSTAGE STAMPS	1	3 00	3 00					
	" 2	RAILWAY FARES - M.SMITH (CHEF)	2	— 70		— 70				
	" 3	STRING AND PENCIL SHARPENERS	3	1 05			1 05			
	" 3	GUEST TAXI - Mr JONES Rm.17	4	1 05					1 05	
	" 3	EXCESS POSTAGE ON PARCEL	5	— 12	— 12					
	" 4	LIFEBOAT DAY - CHARITY	6	— 25						— 25
	" 6	ERASERS, BIROS,	7	1 35			1 35			
	" 6	DELIVERY MAN'S TIP	8	— 30						— 30
	" 6	CARRIAGE ON PARCEL	9	— 15				— 15		
				7 97	3 12	— 70	2 40	— 15	1 05	— 55
	" 7	BALANCE	c/d	7 03	£ 8	£ 9	£ 10	£ 11	Each item is debited separately to guests' account on tabular ledger	£ 12
15 00				15 00						
7 03	JAN 8	BALANCE	b/d	— —						
7 97	" 8	REIMBURSING CASH		— —						

Figure 5.9 *Petty cash book (analysed)*

5.4   THE TABULAR LEDGER

In hotel and catering accounts, the sales day book is replaced by the visitors' tabular ledger, which is simply a form of analysed or columnar book-keeping. Several different types of tabular ledger are in use, but always the basic principle is the same. It consists of a sheet for each day which has numerous analysis columns — the headings of these will depend on the requirements of the hotel. Guests' bills are written up daily from the duplicate vouchers which are debited to the visitors' tabular ledger and it follows that the balances shown on the guests' bills must correspond with the balances in the visitors' tabular ledger.

Example of vertical tabular ledger (see Fig. 5.10)

Column
1   Room No.
2   Name of guest — a line through means departure.
3   Terms, e.g. room & breakfast or fully inclusive (en pension).
    Rate — Charge per person.
4   B/F — Balance brought forward.
5   Apartments — Charge for apartment per night.
6   Pension — Charge for inclusive meals (i.e. breakfast, luncheon, afternoon tea, dinner).
7   Breakfast — Charge for any chance breakfasts.
8   Luncheons — Charge for any chance luncheons.
9   Afternoon teas — Charge for any chance afternoon teas.
10   Dinners — Charge for any chance dinners.
11   Early tea — Charge to guests for early morning teas.
12   Beverages — Charge for any teas, coffees or other beverages.
13   Wines — Charge for any wines at meals.
14   Spirits, liquors — Charge for spirits and wines taken.
15   Beer — Charge for any beers.
16   Minerals — Charge for any minerals.
17   Telephone — Charge for any telephone calls made.
18   VPOs — Visitors paid out — Any monies paid out on behalf of guests.
19   Sundries — Any sundry charges the guest may incur, e.g. laundry, valeting, taxis.
20   Total debits — Total of all charges made to the guest's bill.
21   Cash — Any cash, cheques or payment made by credit cards made by guest.
22   Allowances — Any allowances made to the guest which will be deducted from their bill.
23   Ledger — Any amount which is transferred to a ledger account.
24   Balance c/f — Amounts which are carried forward to the next day's tabular ledger. An amount circled indicates a credit balance.
25   Total credits — Total of all payments, allowances or transfers to ledger.
26   Folio No. & notes — Any ledger folio No. and notes.

To balance the tabular ledger the columns should be added across and down and the total debits should equal the total credits.

Line		501	502	503	504	CHANCE MEALS	501	Silver Tours	Peacock Bar	507	508	509	510	DAILY TOTAL
1	ROOM No.	501	502	503	504		501			507	508	509	510	
2	NAME	Mr. K. James	Mrs S. Horton	Mrs L. Sales	Miss J. Paige		Mr D. Carter	Silver Tours	Peacock Bar	Mrs D. Brown	Mrs E. White	Mrs F. Green	Mrs G. Bluett	
3	No. OF ADULTS	1	2	2	1		1			2	2	2	2	
4	No. OF CHILDREN													
5	TERMS	R+B Bath	Incl. Bath	Incl.	R+B Bath		R+B	Incl.		EXTRAS	EXTRAS	EXTRAS	EXTRAS	
	RATE	21 00	55 00	50 00	21 00		16 00	260 00						DAILY TOTAL
6	B/F	73 50	65 00	105 00	27 00		64 00	260 00						594 50
7	APARTMENTS		20 00	30 00	21 00		16 00	180 00						282 00
8	PENSION							80 00						120 00
9	BREAKFASTS													
10	LUNCHEONS	4 75				28 50	4 75							38 00
11	AFTERNOON TEAS													
12	DINNERS		80	80	7 25	72 50	7 25							87 00
13	EARLY MORNING TEAS	40			40		40							2 80
14	BEVERAGES													
15	WINES		2 20			24 00			65 50	3 40	2 75	3 80	2 75	39 00
16	SPIRITS & LIQUEURS			1 80		5 50	1 10		110 50	1 80	1 10		1 10	77 90
17	BEERS					7 20				2 10				119 80
18	MINERALS				60	2 40	40			40				3 40
19	TELEPHONES	1 50	50								1 70		1 50	6 40
20	VPO's			1 20			Taxi 3 00				2 00			5 00
21	SUNDRIES													
22	TOTAL DEBITS	80 15	123 60	158 80	56 25	140 10	96 50	520 00	176 00	7 70	7 55	3 80	5 35	1375 80
23	CASH	80 15			60 00	140 10			176 00	a/c 1 00				456 25
24	ALLOWANCES													1 00
25	LEDGER							520 00						520 00
26	BALANCE C/F		123 60	158 80	(3 75)		96 50			6 70	7 55	3 80	5 35	398 55
27	TOTAL CREDITS	80 15	123 60	158 80	56 25	140 10	96 50	520 00	176 00	7 70	7 55	3 80	5 35	1375 80
28	FOLIO No.	Access Card						Silver Tours Ltd.						

Figure 5.10 Example of vertical tabular ledger

MONTHLY SUMMARY SHEET

Date	Apartments £	Pension £	Breakfasts £	Luncheons £	Afternoon teas £	Dinner £	Early morning teas £	Beverages £	Wines £	Spirits and liqueurs £	Beers and minerals £	Telephone £	Sundries £	Total £	Allowances £	Net total £
19— June 1																
2																
3																
4																
5																
6																
7																
8																
9																
10																
11																
12																
13																
14																
15																
16																
17																
18																
19																
20																
21																
22																
23																
24																
25																
26																
27																
28																
29																
30																
Total																

These totals should add up to this total
These allowances should be taken away
to give this total

Figure 5.11 *Monthly summary sheet*

Notes
1. The line through 501 indicates that Mr R. James departed after lunch settling his account of £80.15 by Access credit card. Room 501 was relet later in the day and this would be entered in red on the 'Tab' to indicate a relet.
2. By paying £60 cash Miss J. Paige's room 504 would have overpaid by £3.75. Therefore, her account would be in credit and ringed to indicate a credit balance carried forward.
3. Any cash taken in the restaurant from chance sales would be entered on the tabular ledger under the 'chance meals' column, and also shown as cash received.
4. For the 'Silver Tours' package tour a column would show the inclusive charge to be made to 'Silver Tours Ltd' for the apartments and meals. That account would be transferred to a ledger account and a statement sent to 'Silver Tours Ltd' for payment. Separate accounts would be opened for the members of the party (rooms 507–510) for any extra charges they would incur and settlement of these accounts would be made by the individuals.
5. Peacock Bar — Any monies taken in the bar would be paid in; the takings from wines, spirits and beers would be entered in the appropriate column and the cash would be entered as paid in.

    From the daily tabular ledger sheets monthly summary sheets are prepared (see Fig. 5.11).

Chance trade

A 'chance' guest or 'walk-in' is a person who has no reservation. 'Chance' trade is the term used also to describe the business which comes from guests who take meals or drinks in the hotel which are not included in the terms of their reservation and has to be charged to them. 'Chance' business comes also from non-residents who have meals or drinks in the hotel and pay cash. Details of 'chance' business is entered on the tabular ledger in the appropriate column, i.e. breakfast, luncheons, afternoon teas, dinners, bars, and any cash received is shown in the cash received column.

Credit sales

If the hotel has regular restaurant credit customers to whom a monthly statement is sent, it is usual to keep a sales day book for the restaurant which is posted to the ledger. (See Fig. 5.12).

Special functions

If the establishment has substantial special function business, e.g. banquets, weddings, dances, dinners, conferences, etc., it is usual to open a separate special functions day book which is posted to a composite special functions debtors account in the ledger.

Deposits in advance

Any deposits received in advance are entered in the cash book and posted to a composite account in the ledger in which is entered all deposits received. When the guest arrives the deposit is transferred (Dr) from the advance deposit account in the ledger to the guest's account on the tabular ledger (Cr).

Sales day book — restaurant

Bill number	Date	Account to be debited	Folio number	£	
8216	JUNE 1	SALTDEAN SAILING CLUB	L.30	18	20
8310	" 1	BELL ENGINEERING CO.	L.12	8	10
8418	" 3	L. WHITELAW, ESQ.	L.32	7	20
8430	" 4	BELL ENGINEERING LTD	L.12	6	10
8511	" 7	MARSH MOTORS LTD.	L.15	15	10
8561	" 8	LOW & WHITE LTD.	L.14	25	20
		Sales account credited £	L.42	£79	90

Specimen bill

Number 8561

Table number	6	Date 8.6.19—
Number of covers	4	
Waiter number	21	

		£	P
Luncheons	Table d'hôte 4 × £4·50	18	00
Coffee	4 × 40	1	60
Apéritifs	2 × 55	1	10
Wines	1 bottle Nuits St. George	4	50
Spirits	—		
Sundries	—		

T. Smith
Low & White Ltd

Inclusive of Value Added Tax
Total £ 25 20

Figure 5.12 *Diagram illustrating posting of charged restaurant bill to restaurant sales day book*

5.5   CONTROL ACCOUNTS

A control account is constructed apart from the system of double entry. It is a device which enables a clerk to balance a section of the ledger, e.g. the sales or purchases, independently in order to check the accuracy of the entries in that section. One of the great advantages of mechanised accounts is that machines accumulate the amount of individual postings as they are made so that the total balance of the ledger can be ascertained each day.

The total balances on the sales ledger (visitors' ledger) will give the total sundry debtors; the total balance of the purchases ledger will give the total of the sundry creditors.

Dr.				Purchases Ledger Control A/C			Cr.
19 . .			£	19 . .			£
Jan. 1	Balances	b/d	400.00	Jan. 31	Returns		30.00
				31	Cash		
31	Purchases		570.00		Discount		320.00
				31	Balances	c/d	620.00
			£970.00				£970.00
Feb. 1	Balances	b/d	620.00				

Figure 5.13

5.6   THE TRIAL BALANCE

This is a list of the balances extracted from the ledger at the conclusion of posting. It provides a check on the arithmetical accuracy of the double entry, but it is not proof that the transactions have been correctly recorded.

Errors a trial balance will show

1.   The cash book balanced incorrectly.
2.   Incorrect additions of sales, purchases or returns books.
3.   An entry posted to the wrong side of an account.
4.   An incorrect amount posted to the ledger.
5.   Discounts transferred incorrectly.
6.   A debit or credit omitted in posting.
7.   A combined journal entry added incorrectly.

Errors a trial balance will not show

1.   Errors of omission — An entry completely omitted from all books.
2.   Errors of commission — Entry posted to the wrong account.
3.   Errors of principle — A purchase treated as a sale; a receipt treated as a payment; returns in treated as returns out; an asset treated as an expense.
4.   Errors in original entry — Wrong amount entered in book of first entry.
5.   Compensating errors — Two errors of the same amount, one on each side of the ledger.
6.   Error of duplication — The same transaction entered twice.

Methods of locating errors in trial balance

1. Check ledger to see if every account, including the cash and bank, is in the trial balance.
2. Check the balance of the cash book.
3. Check additions in the subsidiary books of first entry.
4. Add credit and debit sides of the trial balance, take one from the other, halve the difference and check if any item of this amount is on the wrong side.
5. Check posting of discounts.
6. Check additions in ledger.
7. Check folio columns for any posting omitted.
8. Check each item in ledger ticking the entry in both ledger and book of first entry.
9. Look for slides, e.g. £17.93 written as £17.39.

5.7 BANKING AND CASH CONTROL

The main cash book

Most businesses keep most of their cash in the bank for security reasons, and only a certain amount of cash is kept on the premises for 'floats' or office cash. Some payments are made by cash and some by cheque; therefore, to keep control of the cash on the premises and in the bank, a three-column cash book is used (see Fig. 5.14(a).

On the debit side of the cash book all amounts of cash received are shown in the cash column, and all amounts banked are shown in the bank column. On the credit side all payments made in cash are shown in the cash column and payments made by cheque are shown in the bank column. If any cash is transferred from the office to the bank or a cheque is cashed for office use a *contra* entry is made, which means an entry is made on the
debit and credit side of the cash book showing the transfer and c is written in the folio column.

Trade discount is an allowance made off the catalogue or list price of goods given by a wholesaler to a retailer. It is shown on invoices only.

Cash discount is an allowance off a debt given to encourage prompt payment. Any discount allowed to a customer is entered in the discount allowed column of the cash book; and any discount received from a supplier is entered in the discount received column of the cash book (see Fig. 5.14).

Cash book example (see Fig. 5.14)

19—			£
Jan.	1	Balance of office cash	80.00
„	1	Balance at bank	1500.00
„	2	Paid cheque to L. Williams & Co.	350.00
„	3	Bought provisions for cash	50.00
„	4	Cashed cheque for office use	20.00
„	4	Cash sales	120.00
„	4	Paid wages in cash	40.00
„	7	Cash sales	100.00
„	8	Paid cash into bank	130.00
„	8	Paid B. Jones his account of £60 less 5% cash discount	

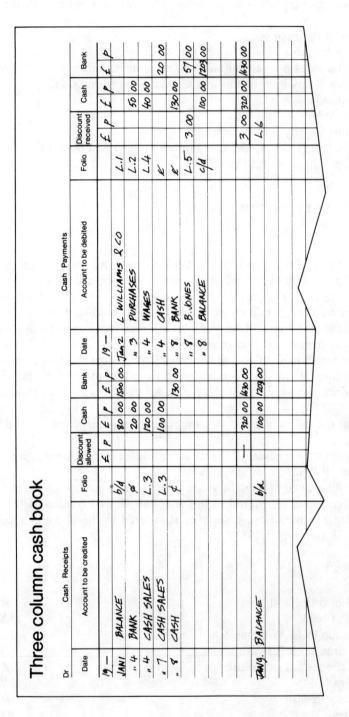

Figure 5.14(a) *Three column cash book*

L. WILLIAMS & Co.–1

Date	Details	Folio	£	p	Date	Details	Folio	£	p
Jan 2	Cash	C.B.I	350	00					

PURCHASES–2

Date	Details	Folio	£	p	Date	Details	Folio	£	p
Jan 3	Cash	C.B.I	50	00					

SALES–3

Date	Details	Folio	£	p	Date	Details	Folio	£	p
					Jan 4	Cash	C.B.I	120	00
					Jan 7	Cash	C.B.I	100	00

WAGES–4

Date	Details	Folio	£	p	Date	Details	Folio	£	p
Jan 4	Cash	C.B.I	40	00					

B. JONES–5

Date	Details	Folio	£	p	Date	Details	Folio	£	p
Jan 8	Cash	C.B.I	57	00					
Jan 8	Discount	C.B.I	3	00					

DISCOUNTS RECEIVED–6

Date	Details	Folio	£	p	Date	Details	Folio	£	p
					Jan 8	Total Discounts	C.B.I	3	00

Figure 5.14(b) *Posting to ledger from cash book (Fig. 5.14(a))*

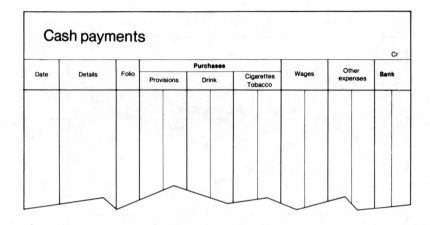

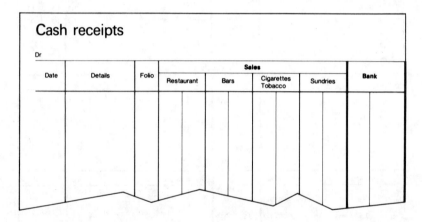

Figure 5.15   *Cash book (analysed)*

Analysed cash books

Many small hotels and similar establishments keep analysed cash books where the income and expenditure is analysed. This provides information and data and is useful when preparing final accounts (Fig. 5.15).

Bank reconciliation statements

Periodically a business will receive a bank statement from the bank. This is a copy of the customers' accounts in the books of the bank. In theory the entries should correspond with the entries in the cash book of the business (but on opposite sides); in practice, however, it is found that the cash book balance and the balance as shown on the bank statement rarely agree. A bank reconciliation statement is therefore prepared to show how the difference has arisen. This difference may be brought about by:

1.   Cheques credited in the cash book but not yet presented for payment to the bank.
2.   Cheques debited in the cash book but not yet paid in or credited by the bank.
3.   Items appearing on the bank statement but not entered in the cash book such as bank charges, standing orders, interest charged on overdrafts or bank giro credits.

Example 1 (an account showing a credit balance with the bank)

	£
Balance as per bank statement 31 March 19—	1238.00
Bank charges debited by bank	4.50
Cheques drawn but not yet presented	71.50
Cheques not yet credited by bank	230.00
Bank giro credit	25.00

Bank reconciliation statement
as at 31 March, 19—

	£	£
Balance as per bank statement (Cr)		1238.00
Add Cheques not yet credited	230.00	
Bank charges	4.50	234.50
		1472.50
Less Cheques not yet presented	71.50	
Bank giro credit	25.00	96.50
Balance as per cash book (Dr)		£1376.00

Example 2 (account showing an overdraft — debit balance with the bank)

	£
Balance as per bank statement 31 March 19— (Dr)	128.00
Cheques not yet credited	44.00
Bank charges debited by bank	5.00
Cheques not yet presented	56.00
Interest on overdraft	2.00

Bank reconciliation statement
as at 31 March 19—

	£	£
Balance as per bank statement (Dr)		128.00
Add Cheques not yet presented		56.00
		184.00
Less Cheques not yet credited	44.00	
Bank charges	5.00	
Interest on overdraft	2.00	51.00
Balance as per cash book (Cr)		£133.00

Banking

The bank provides many services for their customers besides keeping their money safe; it provides convenient means of making payments by cheque and also submits a clear statement of their customer's account at fixed intervals.

Types of bank account

1   *Current account.* Cash is paid in, drawn out or paid away to a third party by means of cheques. No interest is paid on a current account by most banks.

2 *Deposit account.* Sums of money not required for immediate use can be put into a deposit account on which the bank will pay interest.

Types of cheque

Bearer cheques
The amount stated can be paid over the counter to the person presenting the cheque.

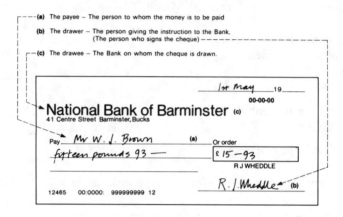

Figure 5.16 *Parties to a cheque*

Order cheques
The cheque is made payable to a specific person.

Open cheques
Cash may be given by the bank.

Crossed cheques
The holder cannot cash the cheque, but only pay it in to a bank account, or savings bank, or assign it to a third party. A crossed cheque therefore gives some protection against fraud if it falls into the wrong hands. It has two parallel lines drawn across its face.

If a bank disobeys the instructions in a special crossing, then it becomes liable to the owner if any loss is suffered.

Not negotiable
A cheque is a 'negotiable instrument'. Accepting money or negotiable instruments in good faith does not render the acceptor liable to return them if they turn out to have been obtained illegally. But any persons accepting a cheque marked 'not negotiable' must take it subject to any defect in title. This means that if the cheque has been stolen or obtained by fraud, they will have to suffer the loss if they accept it.

Example 1
Mr Jason, a small hotelier, accepts a crossed cheque marked 'not negotiable' from a guest calling himself B. Smythe for £10 in payment of his bill. Unkown to the hotelier,

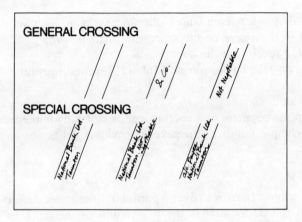

Figure 5.17 *Crossings on cheques*

the cheque had been stolen and the signature forged. As the guest calling himself Mr Smythe did not have legal title to the cheque, he could not give legal title to the hotelier; therefore, the cheque would not be paid and the hotelier would suffer the loss. (This emphasises the point that before accepting any cheque proof of identity should be sought.)

Example 2
Mr Williams had no bank account and received a crossed cheque marked 'not negotiable' payable to himself for £15. He asks a hotelier if he will accept the cheque in payment of a bill for £15. As Mr Williams has legal title to the cheque, and provided that he endorses it (signs his name on the back), a good title can be passed on to the hotelier and it can be paid into the hotelier's bank account.

Correction of a mistake on a cheque
If a correction has been made on a cheque, the correction should be signed in full by the drawer.

Dishonoured cheques
A bank dishonours a cheque by stamping it 'RD' which means 'refer to drawer'. The bank can do this for any of the following reasons:

(a) insufficient funds in the account of the drawer;
(b) no signature;
(c) words and figures do not agree;
(d) incorrect signature;
(e) mutilated cheque;
(f) stale cheque (more than six months old);
(g) if the drawer dies.

Cheques requiring endorsement
Endorsement consists of the signature of the payee on the back of the cheque. Cheques requiring endorsement are:

(a)   cheques payable to a person who wishes to pass it through another person's bank account, e.g. if they have no bank account of their own;
(b)   cheques with a receipt on the back;
(c)   drafts drawn on HM Paymaster and Inland Revenue warrants.

Stopping payment on a cheque
A drawer can stop the payment of a cheque lost or stolen by immediately informing the bank, giving the cheque number and payee, providing it has not already been passed through a bank.

Loans and overdrafts
A loan is a sum of money borrowed over a period of time at a certain rate of interest. An overdraft is when the customer has the permission of the bank to overdraw his/her account by a set sum on which the bank will charge interest.

Traders' credits (Bank Giro)
Instead of drawing individual cheques for each creditor, a trader may give his bank a list of creditors to be paid with the name of the bank where each creditor has his account. The bank then transfers the appropriate amounts to the creditors' banks, and deducts the total amount paid from the trader's account.

Accepting a cheque
A receptionist accepting cheques from a guest should note the following points.
1.   The cheque must not exceed the limit set by the banker's card, i.e. £50 unless the management personally accept the responsibility of authorising cheques over this amount.
2.   The date must not be a future one, nor must it be out of date (more than six months).
3.   The words and figures must agree, if either has been altered the alteration must be signed by the drawer.
4.   The hotel must be named as the payee.
5.   The guest must sign the cheque.
6.   The guest should sign his name and address on the back for reference and identification and the cheque should be supported if possible by a credit card or cheque guarantee card.

Special clearance of a cheque
If the cashier wishes to verify if a cheque is acceptable, a telephone call to the hotel's bank giving details of the cheque, the drawer's name, and the branch on which it is to be drawn, the bank will make contact with the drawer's bank and establish whether the cheque is acceptable. The cost of the telephone call is usually passed on to the guest.

5.8 CREDIT CARDS

The method of making payment by use of credit cards is now quite commonplace. They are accepted by most hotels, shops and garages. The banks or organisations that issue them guarantee payment of bills run up by the credit card holder up to a certain limit.

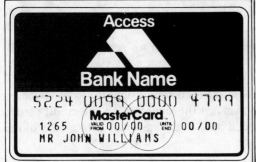

Figure 5.18 *Credit cards (reproduced with permission)*

Accepting payment by credit card

When accepting settlement of a bill by credit card the cashier should:

1. Check that the total amount of the bill does not exceed the 'floor limit', which is the maximum amount of credit allowed without getting special authorisation. The major credit card companies have a direct telephone system and by telephoning the number and quoting the credit card number an approval or disapproval code number will be given to the caller.
2. The cashier completes a sales voucher, which is usually in triplicate, for the amount due.
3. The credit card is presented by the customer to the cashier who checks the details, in particular the expiry date of the card.
4. An imprint of the details on the card is made on the sales voucher.
5. The cashier should retain the credit card whilst the customer signs the sales voucher.
6. The signature on the voucher is checked against the signature on the credit card.
7. If all is satisfactory the credit card is handed back to the customer with a copy of the sales voucher and a receipted bill.

Accounting for payment by credit card

Credit card companies operate on a commission basis. Sales vouchers for payment made by the bank credit cards such as Access and Barclaycard are treated as cash. The vouchers are paid into the bank on a separate paying-in slip and the hotel's account would be credited with the amount owed less the credit card company's commission.

  Sales vouchers relating to other credit card companies such as American Express, Diners Club International, Carte Blanche, etc. are dealt with in a different manner. These vouchers are collected together and despatched with an account to the respective credit card companies, who will then pay the amount owing less commission, direct to the hotel. In the accounts system the cash and discount received from credit card sales would be debited in the cash book and credited to the sales account.

5.9 TRAVELLER'S CHEQUES

These can be in sterling or in another currency. The guest must sign the traveller's cheque in front of the cashier and this signature must correspond with the one already on the cheque. If there is any doubt, the cashier should tactfully try to obtain proof of identity, e.g. passport or driving licence. Lists of stolen or lost traveller's cheques are circulated to hotels and the cashier should consult these lists discreetly when dealing with traveller's cheques.

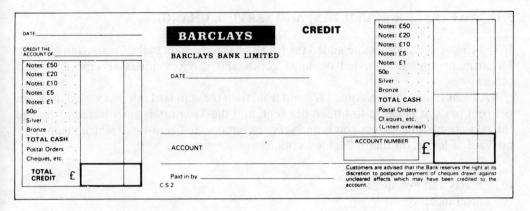

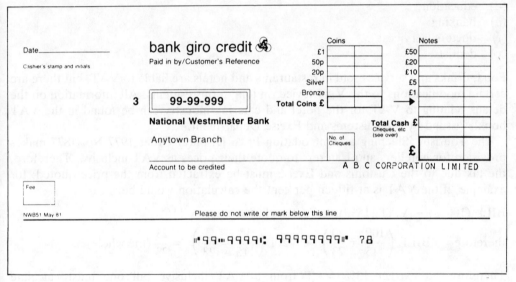

Figure 5.19 *Paying-in slip (reproduced with permission)*

5.10 PAYING IN (Fig. 15)

Paying-in books are issued by the bank and are stamped with the name and number of the establishment's account at the bank (Fig. 5.19). When handling or checking cash the cashier should exercise particular care. Separate the £50, £20, £10, £5, £1 notes and stack them face upwards in the same direction. £1, 50p, 20p, 10p, 5p coins should be stacked in their respective denominations; 2p, 1p or ½p coins should also be stacked into piles for easy checking and counting, then bundled into the appropriate cash bags supplied by the bank. Bank credit card vouchers and traveller's cheques and foreign currencies are entered on separate paying-in slips.

The paying-in slips are completed and the cash and slips are handed in to the bank cashier who will check that they are all correct, stamp the counterfoil and retain the paying-in slip. The establishment's account is then credited with the amount paid in.

5.11   VAT (VALUE ADDED TAX) AND SERVICE CHARGE

In the United Kingdom value added tax (VAT) has to be paid to the Customs and Excise Department, and it is levied on most goods and services unless specifically stated otherwise.

   VAT was introduced in April 1973 and from then the standard rate has varied from ten per cent to eight per cent to fifteen per cent, and the Treasury is empowered to change the rate at any time. Some goods and services are deemed zero-rated which means that no VAT is levied on them. Such exceptions are:

(a)   most foods;
(b)   books and newspapers;
(c)   insurance;
(d)   education;
(e)   banking;
(f)   doctors' services;
(g)   dentists.

Food, drinks and services sold in restaurants and hotels are liable to VAT, but there are certain modifications to the VAT levied on long-term residents. All information on the details relating to VAT for the hotel and catering industry can be found in the VAT booklet issued by the Customs and Excise Department.

   The Tourism (Sleeping accommodation Price Display) Order 1977 No. 1877 makes provision for hoteliers and Caterers to quote their prices as VAT inclusive. Therefore, the tax due to the Customs and Excise must be extracted from the price quoted; for example, if the VAT is at fifteen per cent the calculation would be:

BILL (100%) + VAT (15%) = VAT inclusive price = 115%

$$\text{therefore} \quad \text{BILL} \left(\frac{100}{115} = \frac{20}{23} \right) + \text{VAT} \left(\frac{15}{115} = \frac{3}{23} \right) = \frac{23}{23} \text{ (the whole)}$$

Therefore, to extract 15% VAT from a VAT inclusive bill one must calculate $\frac{3}{23}$ by multiplying by 3 and dividing by 23.

Example 1 Bill VAT inclusive

$$
\begin{array}{r}
£25.30 \\
\times\, 3 \\
\hline
75.90 \\
\div\, 23 \\
\hline
\text{VAT} = \quad 3.30 \\
\hline
\end{array}
$$

Check

Bill (VAT exclusive)	£22.00
Add 15% VAT	3.30
Bill VAT inclusive	£25.30

Service charge

Any service charge added to a bill is subject to VAT. If a bill is quoted as service charge and VAT included the VAT is extracted first (see example) then the service charge is extracted.

Example 2 Bill VAT exclusive £22.00

Bill + Service charge 10% =

$$\left(\frac{100}{110}\right) + \left(\frac{10}{110} = \frac{1}{11}\right) = \frac{110}{110}$$

To extract service charge @ 10% divide by 11

$$£22.00$$
$$\div 11$$
$$\text{Service charge } £\ 2.00$$

Check

Bill (exclusive of service charge) £20.00	
+ 10% service charge	+ 2.00
Bill inclusive	£22.00

If the service charge or value added tax rate should change the basic calculation would be the same:

Example 3 Service charge at 12%

$$\frac{100^{25}}{112_{28}} + \frac{12^{3}}{112_{28}} = \frac{28}{28}\text{(the whole)}$$

To extract service charge @ 12% find $\frac{3}{28}$; therefore, multiply by 3 and divide by 28.

5.12   FOREIGN CURRENCIES

The hotel can be the authorised agent for foreign currency transactions. The cashier should observe currency regulations and be aware of the rates of exchange, which change daily. Foreign currency is exchanged at the bank and any 'profit on exchange' is entered in the cash received book.

Hotel receptionists dealing with foreign visitors should become conversant with the currencies of other countries and should be able to convert currencies easily and rapidly. The method of converting is simple.

GRAND HOTEL					
Exchange Rates on : Date					
Country	Currency	Rate £1 =	Country	Currency	Rate £1 =
Australia	Dollar		Malta	Pound	
Austria	Schilling		Morocco	Dirham	
Belgium	Franc		New Zealand	Dollar	
Canada	Dollar		Norway	Krona	
Denmark	Krone		Portugal	Escudo	
Eire	Pound		Spain	Peseta	
Finland	Markka		Sweden	Krona	
West Germany	Deutschmark		Switzerland	Franc	
Greece	Drachma		Saudi Arabia	Riyal	
Holland	Guilder		Tunisia	Dinar	
Hongkong	Dollar		Turkey	Lira	
Italy	Lira		USA	Dollar	
Japan	Yen		Yugoslavia	Dinar	

Figure 5.20   *Foreign exchange rate table*

Complete the above table with present day rates.

Example
To convert sterling into foreign currency multiply the amount by the rate of exchange. For example, convert £15 into French Francs (rate: £1 = 11.35 f.).

$$£15 \times 11.35 = 170.25 \text{ francs}$$

To convert foreign currency into sterling divide the amount by the rate of exchange. For example, 170.25 francs divided by 11.35 gives the sterling equivalent.

$$\frac{170.25}{11.35} = £15$$

5.13   MECHANISED ACCOUNTING

Advantages of office machines

1. *Increased speed.* Time and labour can be saved by simultaneous posting in one operation (about five times faster than posting by hand).
2. *Greater accuracy.* Some of the human errors can be reduced, especially in calculations.
3. *Improved records.* Bills prepared by machine are neater and more legible, therefore more helpful to the staff and more pleasing to the customer.
4. *Elimination of tedious repetitive work* such as casting and balancing.
5. *Information for management* can be quickly and easily produced.

Types of office accounting machines

1. *Adding machines.* These can be either electric or manually operated and are useful for checking additions and prelisting.
2. *Calculating machines.* There are numerous types, nearly all electronic, and these machines can perform all four basic arithmetical functions: addition, subtraction, multiplication and division. They are useful for invoice checking, valuation of stock, conversion of foreign currencies and other control calculations.
3. *Accounting/book-keeping machines.* There are numerous types, which are a combination of a calculating machine and typewriter. Many businesses use accounting machines for ledger posting, payroll, receipt writing, stock records, sales analysis, cost analysis and various statistical reports.

Computerised guest accounting for hotels

A well-known Minister of Technology defined information technology (IT) as the use of computers, microelectronics and telecommunications designed to help us produce, store, obtain and send information in the form of pictures, words or numbers more reliably, quickly and economically. Without a doubt 'information technology' has become the most rapidly developing area of industrial and business activity in the Western world.

There are many large and reputable organisations in the computer servicing industry producing:

Hardware.
This means the physical components of computers, including the minicomputers, microcomputers and integrated systems and attachments to the computers.

Software.
This means computer programs, including the specially designed programs on various types of disc, e.g. hard discs, floppy discs which are used in conjunction with the hardware.

Floppy disc
So called because it is a flexible disc, 5¼ inches in diameter, with limited capacity. The surface must not be touched and it must be stored in a cool dry place away from electrical equipment because it is magnetic.

Hard disc
It is not possible to remove a hard disc. It is totally sealed and spins at very high speeds and can therefore retrieve and store information very quickly. It is the equivalent to four floppy discs.

It is not possible to go into the details of the technology involved or to mention all the companies now producing hardware and software for the hotel industry, but to name a few:

Figure 5.21 *NCR Quicksilver*

The NCR Quicksilver (Fig. 5.21)

This is a guest accounting control system with a front desk terminal:

Special features
1. A simplified programmable keyboard with a ten-key numerical arrangement, multiple departmental keys, settlement keys and an assortment of special function keys.
2. Departmental keys which enable separate totals for guests services, room charge, restaurant and bar services, valet, laundry, garage and others.
3. Cashiers' keys which identify the cashier or shift which is printed on the folios (bills) vouchers and audit journals.
4. Room rates are stored in the computer's memory and when the cashier enters the room rate code and presses the room rate look-up key; the terminal locates the rate in its memory, prints it on the folio and updates the totals.
5. Room number and balance can be verified. An automatic check digit is generated every time a new balance is printed. When the room number and balance pick up check digits are entered they are verified electronically and if incorrect the terminal will reject the entire entry as invalid thus eliminating a common error in posting to guest's folio.
6. A posting error can be corrected by using a correction or void key.
7. Advance payments can be transferred to an advance reservation deposit by using the transfer debit and credit keys.
8. Package rates — when special rates are offered to travel agents or tour operators, the computer can distribute the charges to their respective departments. This information is printed on the audit journal but only the total package prints on the guest's folio.
9. The trial balance feature provides the automatic accummulation of debit and credit balance in separate totals.

Sweda L–45–30 (Fig. 5.22)

The Sweda is an electronic hotel posting machine and cash register which has been specially tailored for the hotel industry. It produces clear legible bills for the guest, fast accurate operations for reception and security and information for the management.

Figure 5.22 *Sweda L45–30 (reproduced with the permission of Sweda International)*

Special features
1. The departmental digits cover all the services such as laundry, telephone, valet, restaurant, bars, coffee shops, newspapers, etc.
2. The keys cover eleven types of payment and eight miscellaneous keys cover the major credit cards, all with programmable limitations to alert the operator when management authorisation must be given to accept vouchers over a certain limit.
3. Three separate cashier totals ABD.
4. Up to 512 room balances may be stored, including 'split rooms' where two individuals in a room want separate bills.
5. Currency conversions on ten rates of exchange.
6. Debit and credit balances.
7. VAT system where VAT can be added or extracted.
8. Folio printer with four columns: reference, debit, credit, balancing for easy reference (Fig. 5.23).

Figure 5.23 *Guest folio (bill) (reproduced with the permission of Sweda International)*

9. Alphanumerical display to alert cashier when to insert vouchers.
10. Trial balance to facilitate hotel accounting.
11. A training mode for cashier training.

Abbreviations used in machine accounting

#	Number
AD	Advance deposit
BAL	Balance or balance key
C BAL	Credit balance
CID	Cash in drawer
C/L	City ledger
Comp	Complimentary or compulsory
D BAL	Debit balance

Dept	Department
IRC	Inter-register communications
MAX	Maximum
MIN	Minimum
P BAL	Previous balance
PLU	Price look up
ROOM #	Room number pick up key
STTL	Sub total

Hoskyns computer systems (Fig. 5.24)

The Hoskyns Group have developed a range of computers specially tailored to the hotel industry.

5.14   HARDWARE

The range of hardware equipment available depends on the special requirements of the hotel and the volume of business and which software modules are installed.

Features
(a)   the processor;
(b)   the memory configuration to meet the individual requirements;
(c)   discs — Winchester hard discs are used;
(d)   streamers — used to back up the Winchester disc — software is distributed using tape streamer cassettes;
(e)   visual display units;
(f)   printers;
(g)   terminals in restaurants, switchboard, porters desks, housekeeping office to post charges direct to the guest's account or in the case of the housekeeper to enquire or update on the room status;
(h)   communications — with central reservations or other departments.

5.15   SYSTEMS (SOFTWARE)

Systems can be designed to cover the complete guest cycle and management control features:

Reservations
(a)   individual and group bookings;
(b)   travel agents, block allocations;
(c)   room pre-allocation;
(d)   deposit requests, and confirmation letters;
(e)   commissions;
(f)   statistical analysis.

Figure 5.24 *Hoskyns guest accounting system (reproduced with the permission of the Hoskyns Group Ltd)*

Rooms Management
(a) room status displays;
(b) arrivals and departures list.

Registration
(a) registration;
(b) key cards;
(c) individual and group check in;
(d) guest messages;
(e) baggage control.

Guest accounting
(a) advance deposits;
(b) multiple folios;
(c) automatic apartment charging;
(d) analysis of inclusive terms;
(e) tour accounts;
(f) function accounts;
(g) flexible rate charges;
(h) VAT analysis.

Cashier departures
(a) bill settlement and any other payments in any combination of cash, cheques, traveller's cheques or credit cards with automatic sterling conversion;
(b) foreign currency exchange using up to sixteen present rates;
(c) automatic posting to guests' accounts from other terminals; tax analysis;
(d) detailed analysis of cash drawer totals, cashier totals and banking totals;
(e) fully itemised receipts for guests;
(f) baggage control.

Control office
(a) comprehensive revenue analysis;
(b) full transaction auditing;
(c) sales analysis.

Management information
(a) forward analysis of rooms, revenue sleepers;
(b) guest credit control;
(c) statistics;
(d) budgetary control;
(e) guest history sales analysis.

5.16 PROGRESS TEST QUESTIONS

1. Give two examples of each of the following.
   (a) a nominal account;
   (b) a personal account;
   (c) a real account.
2. J. Chalan is a supplier to the Hotel Unicorn. From the following information write up his account as it would appear in the books of the hotel:

		£
Mar. 1	Balance owing to J. Chalan	72.00
Mar. 2	Goods supplied by J. Chalan invoice No. 326	35.50
Mar. 3	Cheque sent to J. Chalan in settlement of balance owing 1 March less 5% cash discount	
Mar. 4	Credit note No. 121 received from J. Chalan in respect of goods returned by the hotel	2.30
Mar. 4	Goods supplied by J. Chalan invoice No. 420	41.50
	Balance the account as at 5 March.	

3. From the following information prepare a bank reconciliation statement as at 31 March: the bank statement shows a credit balance of £298.75. Cheques drawn but not yet presented for payment £131.00; standing orders shown as paid on the bank statement but not entered in cash book £82.00; cheques entered in cash book but not yet paid into the bank £64.00. What does the cash book balance show?
4. Explain what is meant by an error of commission; an error of omission; and an error of principle.
5. In which book of first entry would you enter the following business documents:
   (a) a purchase invoice;
   (b) a credit note from a supplier;
   (c) a petty cash voucher?
6. Explain the difference between a current account and a deposit account at the bank.
7. Draw a specimen cheque, complete it and name the payee, drawer and drawee.
8. Explain what is meant by endorsing a cheque and say when it is necessary to endorse a cheque.
9. Explain what you understand by the 'imprest system' of keeping petty cash.
10. Enter the particulars of the guests listed below who are in residence at the Atlas Hotel on an analysed visitors tabular ledger. Close and balance the TAB as if it were the end of the day's business, adding and reconciling all totals:

Tariff for the Atlas Hotel

Room and breakfast	£16.50 (inclusive of breakfast, £2.50 per person)
Inclusive terms	£25.00
Private bathroom	£5.00 per night
Early morning tea	50p
Morning coffee	60p
Luncheon (table d'hôte)	£4.75
Dinner	£7.00

Note:

(a)   Terms are charged daily in advance or for new arrivals immediately upon arrival.

(b)   Inclusive terms cover room, breakfast, luncheon, afternoon tea, dinner.

(c)   All prices are inclusive of service charge and VAT.

(d)   Newspapers to be listed under VPOs.

Guests in residence

Room	Terms	Name	Amount b/f
301	Incl. (bath)	Mr & Mrs S. Brown	£148.10
303	Incl. (bath)	Rev W. Ault	£ 48.70
304	R & B (bath)	Mr & Mrs T. Long	£102.75
306	Incl.	Mr R. Williams	£ 42.50

List of transactions

0715   Early morning tea to all residents. Newspapers Room 303 — 20p, 306 — 40p.

0720   Telephone calls Room 301 — 75p, 306 — 50p.

0730   VPO Room 306 for dry cleaning £2.50.

0830   Breakfast to all residents.
         12 chance breakfasts.

0900   Allowance for correction of errors on yesterday's TAB, Room 301 over-charge of 55p on lounge drinks.

0930   Departure Room 301. Mr Brown pays by American Express less £40 deposit paid in advance.

1000   Room 303 pays £25 cash on account.

1100   Morning coffee to all residents.

1130   Arrival Mr & Mrs L. Summers given Room 301. Terms room & breakfast (bath).

1130   Mr R. Williams, Room 306, checks out. Account to Amcot Ltd.

1300   Lunches Room 301 — 2 lunches, 2 coffees, wine £1.25
         Chance lunches £47.50
         Chance coffees £6.00
         Chance wines £8.50

1400   Arrival of Silver Tours Party. Terms £160 room and breakfast.
         Rooms allocated Mr & Mrs Black   Room 308
                               Mr & Mrs White   Room 309
                               Mr & Mrs Green   Room 310
                               Mr & Mrs Violet   Room 311

1600   Afternoon tea to all residents

1600   Telephone calls: Room 308 — £2.00
                               309 — £1.50
                               310 — £1.20
                               311 — £1.30

1800   Lounge bar pays in £92.50

11. Complete the following table:

(a)

Bill Inclusive	Less 15% VAT	Total	Less 12½% Service charge	Bill Exclusive
£	£	£	£	£
21.50				
33.80				
14.40				
17.40				
26.50				
19.30				
18.60				
24.40				
12.30				
9.20				
Totals				

(b)

Catalogue Price	Less Trade Discount @	Invoice Price	Less Cash Discount @	Net Total
£	%	£	%	£
4.18	10		2½	
5.22	15		5	
12.40	12½		1¼	
18.30	17½		2½	
26.80	25		1¼	
Totals				

12. What do you understand by the terms:
    (a) hardware;
    (b) software;
    (c) hard discs;
    (d) floppy discs.
13. What are some of the advantages of mechanised accounting.
14. List some of the features of:
    (a) the NCR 2251;
    (b) the Sweda I–45–30.
15. List the advantages and disadvantages of a computerised hotel accounting system.

6 Business practice

In a large transient hotel where the length of stay of the guests averages only two to three nights, the volume of work will probably result in a high degree of specialisation and the tasks that have to be performed by the front office staff will be sub-divided into separate sections. In such hotels the brigade of receptionists would in the main be occupied with the front desk reception duties connected with selling accommodation. In smaller seasonal or residential hotels all the office work could be centralised in the reception office, and during the quiet period on the front desk the receptionist would be expected to carry out the task of maintaining accounting and other records.

However, whether employed by a large, medium or small establishment, the receptionist will be required to have a sound general knowledge of business practice, and, if called upon to do so, must be able to perform competently and efficiently the following tasks:

(a) dealing with correspondence;
(b) handling inward and outward mail;
(c) control of stationery;
(d) filing and maintaining records;
(e) duplicating and photocopying;
(f) maintaining stock-control systems;
(g) control of wages systems and staff records;
(h) preparation of statistics and reports;

as well as various miscellaneous office duties.

6.1 CORRESPONDENCE

Every business letter should be written with the idea of creating a favourable impression in the mind of the reader. A badly constructed letter, crude in style, vague in wording and careless in grammar, will create an unfavourable impression, whereas a well framed letter, clear and concise in wording, indicates efficiency.

To be an effective business correspondent one should have a sound knowledge of English, which includes correct spelling, grammar and punctuation, and also be able to construct sentences so that the exact meaning is conveyed in the fewest possible words. Business terms, definitions and abbreviations should be studied.

Desirable features of a good business letter

1. *Accuracy* — As business letters are usually records of business trans-actions, all details must be scrupulously accurate.

2. *Conciseness* — This means that the message of the letter must be conveyed in as few words as possible, using clear, simple expressions and avoiding the use of any unnecessary phrases.
3. *Grammatical correctness* — In addition to correct spelling, a sound knowledge of the rules of English grammar is essential. It is worth remembering that simple sentences are more likely to be grammatically correct than long, involved ones.
4. *Courtesy* — A business letter is often used to obtain new business or to create goodwill; therefore every letter should convey genuine sincerity and courtesy.
5. *Good layout* — The letter should present an attractive appearance and arrangement. A good letter writer will place in a logical sequence the matter about which he or she intends to write. Each topic should be dealt with in a separate paragraph as paragraphing focuses attention on the important points in their correct order.

6.2 INWARD MAIL

Business letters and enquiries for the attention of the management or various departments should be date stamped, sorted and distributed to the appropriate departments immediately upon arrival.

Mail for guests in residence

Any incoming mail for guests should be sorted and placed in the letter rack. The room numbers are ascertained by using the alphabetical guest list. Large envelopes or packets and registered letters are stored in a separate place and a notification slip (Fig. 6.1) is placed in the appropriate pigeon hole in the letter rack asking the guest to collect it either at the reception desk or enquiry office.

Mail for departed guests

If any mail arrives for guests who have departed, providing they have completed the mail forwarding form (Fig. 6.2) the mail is then readdressed and forwarded. These forms are filed alphabetically, the expiry date carefully noted and systematically cleared out after the expiry date has elapsed. Any mail arriving after that date is marked 'address unknown' and returned to the post office.

Mail for future guests

Mail for guests yet to arrive is sorted into alphabetical order and kept to one side in a separate compartment. The advance bookings diary or chart is checked for the guest's arrival date, a note is made in the diary that mail is awaiting and on the appropriate date it is placed in the letter rack.

Notification slip

Whitecrest Hotel
Whitecrest Road
Dyke Regis, Devon
Telephone Dyke Regis 12561
Telegrams: Crest, Dyke Regis
VAT Registration number 123 4567 89

Mr Mrs Miss   *R. L. Essex*   Date *3 May 19—*

Please collect from the reception/enquiry office:-

1 Registered letter

Figure 6.1 *Mail notification slip*

Mail forwarding form

Whitecrest Hotel
Whitecrest Road
Dyke Regis, Devon
Telephone Dyke Regis 12561
Telegrams: Crest, Dyke Regis
VAT Registration number 123 4567 89

Mr Mrs Miss   Room number
Forwarding address

Expiry date

I undertake to re-imburse the Hotel for any expense incurred in forwarding mail

Signed   Date

Date of re-direction	Description		Postage	

Figure 6.2 *Mail forwarding form*

Registered mail (incoming)

The head porter or head receptionist is usually authorised to sign for registered mail. A separate book is kept to record the date and time of arrival and receipt number. A slip to notify the guest that registered mail is awaiting collection is placed in the letter rack. The letters or packages are kept under lock and key or in the safe and when guests collect them they must sign the record book to indicate that they have taken delivery.

Staff mail

The head porter or housekeeper usually distributes any mail that arrives for residential staff.

Procedure for handling cash or cheques in the mail

1. Any cash received in registered letters must be double-checked by the head receptionist.
2. Uncrossed cheques and postal orders should be crossed immediately or stamped with a 'crossings stamp' to avoid fraud.
3. A checklist should be made of all cash, cheques and postal orders received through the post and handed to the cashier for entry into the appropriate records. The cashier should give a receipt to the receptionist that he or she has taken charge of the money.

OUTWARD MAIL

1. A specified time should be set as a deadline when outgoing mail should be ready if it is to be despatched that day.
2. Regular collections of mail for posting should be made throughout the day; this will ease the pressure and build-up of outgoing mail at the end of the day.
3. All mail should be sorted; if there is any post for overseas, care must be taken that the correct postage stamps are affixed.
4. Any post office receipts for registered mail should be gummed into a special book kept for that purpose.
5. All mail for despatch should be franked if a franking machine is used, or the stamps used entered into the postage book, which should be kept on the imprest system (Fig. 6.3).

Postage book

Value of stamps received	Folio	Date	Names	Address	Value of stamps used
£ p		19–			£ p
£ 5–00	Pc B1	Jan 1	Mm Du Bois	Rue de la Loi, Brussels, Belg.	0 16
		" 1	MR & MRS R JAMES	23 Rushmore Drive, M'head	0 16
		" 1	MRS G HORTON	16 Brede Street, Birmingham	0 24

Figure 6.3 *Postage book*

Business reply-paid cards or envelopes

These cards and envelopes are used for establishing goodwill, advertising purposes and for soliciting business. The sender pays the postage if the recipient sends them back. They must conform to the pattern and standard size laid down by the Post Office. A licence has to be obtained and a deposit paid in advance to cover charges for a reasonable time.

Recorded delivery

If proof of postage is required for sending important documents through the post, the package or letter is taken to the post office, and for an extra charge the delivery will be recorded and a receipt obtained as proof. Compensation up to eighteen pounds is payable for loss or damage. Recorded delivery packets must not be dropped into a letter box.

Expresspost

This involves rapid same day delivery.

Expresspost is a fast messenger collection and delivery service available in London using radio controlled motor cycles and vans. It is also available in certain other large towns and cities. In addition to local services within the particular area, there are also many same day inter-city links between Expresspost centres.

Charges are based on distance.

Royal mail special delivery

This gives extra assurance for first class letter mail.

This service provides delivery by a Post Office messenger for letters and packets arriving at a delivery office on the next working day after posting but too late for normal delivery on that day.

In addition to first class postage a Royal Mail Special Delivery Fee of £1.50 must be paid. A Certificate of Posting will be issued. Items must be posted at post office counters in advance of latest recommended posting times for next working day delivery. The special delivery fee will be refunded to the sender in respect of any item posted in advance of latest recommended posting times which does not receive delivery on the next working day after posting.

Registered mail (outgoing)

Registered mail has to be handed in to the post office, which issues an official receipt. These receipts are gummed into a special book kept for the purpose, as they would have to be produced if a claim for compensation is made. Registration of mail is used when money or valuables are sent through the post. Registered letter envelopes in different sizes can be obtained from the post office, or a stout envelope or package can be used by drawing blue lines across the face before it is handed in to the post office. Registration is not a safeguard against damage and the Post Office will only pay compensation if the contents were adequately packed.

6.4 EQUIPMENT AND MACHINES

Letter and parcel scales

If a letter contains more than one sheet of paper it should be weighed on the letter scales to ensure the correct amount of postage is affixed. All parcels and packets should be weighed on the parcel scales.

Stamp folder

Stamps are easily lost; therefore, it is essential that they are contained in a special folder with separate divisions for each denomination. Stamp folders should be kept under lock and key to avoid pilfering.

Franking machines (Fig. 6.4)

If the volume of mail is high, a franking machine can save a lot of time. A postal franker is a machine which has to be hired or purchased from supplying companies licensed by the Post Office. It stamps on the envelope (or on an adhesive strip) the amount of postage required and the date cancellation mark.

Figure 6.4 *Electronic franking machine (Roneo Alcatel Ltd)*

Advance payment has to be made to the Post Office to cover the value of the postage expected to be used. As the stamp value is printed on the envelope, the amount is reduced on the machine until the machine reaches zero. The machine will then lock and has to be taken back to the post office for further payment. Machine-franked mail must be faced, securely tied in bundles and handed in to the post office. A control card showing the readings of the meter of the franking machine must also be tendered to the post office. Care must be taken that the correct denomination of stamp is printed on the envelopes. First-class and second-class mail should be put through the machine on separate runs. The date stamp must be altered every day, as the Post Office will not accept pre- or post-dated mail.

6.5 FILING AND INDEXING

Filing is a process of systematically classifying and storing records so that they can be produced without unreasonable delay. Indexing is the process required to facilitate the location of records.

The basic principles of a good filing system are as follows.

Compactness and accessibility
Filing cabinets should not take up too much floor space and be sited so that it is easy to open drawers and get at records.

Simplicity and elasticity
A good filing system should be simple and easy to understand and operate. It should also be capable of expansion if necessary.

Safety and security
Records may have to be kept for reference over a long period of time and therefore they must be adequately protected. Security measures should be taken for the safe custody of confidential and important files; therefore, cabinets should have locks, with the keys kept by a responsible official.

Speed and efficiency
The proof of a good filing system lies in the ease with which records can be found. Speed is essential, as delays are time-wasting and irritating. Filing should be kept up to date. If a file is removed, an 'out' guide with the date and name of the person or department that has taken it should be inserted in its place. The files should be cleared out regularly and out of date records removed and placed in the 'dead files'.

Methods of filing

Flat filing
Documents are placed one on top of the other in drawers or box files. Cabinets with shallow drawers are available for the horizontal files.

Figure 6.5   *Vertical suspension filing (Roneo Alcatel Ltd)*

Vertical filing (Fig. 6.5)
Vertical filing cabinets with up to five drawers are in general use in offices. These drawers are fitted with rails for suspension files. Dividers in filing drawers are called 'guides'. A 'primary guide' shows the main division and a 'special guide' will donate a special section of the files.

Classifications

There are five basic classifications for filing: alphabetical, numerical, geographical, chronological (date order) and subject-matter. The basis of all these systems is the alphabetical filing of names of either persons, places, things or subjects, and even when the system is numerical it requires an alphabetical index.

Alphabetical
Records are filed according to the first letter of the surname and then in the order of the
first letter of the Christian name, for example:

Names	Filed in order
Mr Stanley Fention	Mr Robert Aldridge
Mr Robert Aldridge	Mr Stanley Fention
Mr Stephen Masters	Mr Stephen Masters

Names	Filed in order
Mr William Jones	Mr Arthur Jones
Mr Arthur Jones	Mr George Jones
Mr George Jones	Mr William Jones

Surnames beginning with 'Mac' or 'Mc' are treated as 'Mac' and the next letter in the
name determines the filing position, for example:

Names	Filed in order
MacArthur	McAlpine
McAlpine	MacArthur
MacDonald	MacDonald

The 'Mac' prefix is usually at the beginning of the 'M' filing. The same principle
applies when the prefix is 'Saint' or 'St', 'O'Brien' or 'O'Toole'. Hyphenated names such
as 'Wynne-Jones' should be filed under 'W', but 'Mr S. Gabriel Brown' should be filed
under 'B'. Titles and ranks such as 'Captain', 'Sir', 'Lord', should be disregarded.

Numerical
Documents or files are given numbers and are filed in number order. This system has to
be used in conjuction with an alphabetical index. To locate a particular file it is necessary
to consult the index first, which will give the file number to be located. Copies of bills or
invoices are usually filed in numerical order.

Geographical
In this system the location or address is used as the identifying heading. The arrangement
would be by country, county, town, street, then number. After grouping in geographical
order, then the alphabetical system is used, for example: a document could be filed
under the general heading of Southern Counties, then under the names in alphabetical
order.

Subject-matter
When records are filed under this system it means that all documents relating to the
subject are brought together under one heading, for example:

Staff	Maintenance
Applications for employment	Carpet cleaning contracts
Contracts	Central heating
Salary scales	Lifts maintenance
Training programmes	Window cleaning
Welfare	

Chronological
Any subject matter which is filed in date order.

Indexing

The purpose of an index is to make it easy to locate any record in the system. Indexing can take any of the following forms:

1. *A page* as in the back of a book.
2. *Vertical cards* arranged in drawers or trays (Fig. 6.6).

Figure 6.6 *Vertical cards arranged in drawers or trays (Roneo Alcatel Ltd)*

3. *Strip index* — This is a frame into which strips of stiff card can be inserted. This is only suitable when the information consists of one line only, such as names and addresses (Fig. 6.7).
4. *Wheel index* — This form of card index is arranged around the circumference of a wheel. Many thousands of cards can be attached to one wheel, which makes it a suitable and speedy system for a large volume of records (Fig. 6.8).

Figure 6.7 *Strip index (Roneo Alcatel Ltd)*

Figure 6.8(a) *Wheel index — rotary vertical unit (Rotadex systems Ltd)*

Figure 6.8(b) *Two tier 'Rondofile' (M. Myers & Son Ltd)*

6.6 STATIONERY

Stationery should be stored in a clean and dry cupboard or stockroom, centrally situated. It should be neatly stacked and clearly labelled. Coloured cards should be inserted in stock as a reminder when to re-order. The type of headings and the colour of paper is entirely a matter of choice and a decision of the management.

Paper sizes are standardised and the most commonly used are:

A4 — 210 mm × 297 mm   and
A5 — 210 mm × 148 mm

and the Post Office prefer envelope sizes to be:

(for A4) 235 mm × 121 mm (width)
(for A5) 140 mm × 89 mm (width)

Continuous stationery

Bills, invoices, office forms and memos can be produced in a continuous strip which is divided by perforations so that the forms can be detached. Several copies of each form can be produced by inserting carbon paper or by using 'no carbon required' (NCR) paper. This paper is chemically treated and whatever is written or typed on the top copy, automatically creates a carbon copy on the paper beneath. The continuous stationery can be folded in a zig-zag fashion (which is the most popular); or fan-folded (which is joined end to end or horizontally and folded concertina fashion), or in a continuous roll.

6.7 DUPLICATING AND PHOTOCOPYING

When a large number of copies of the same document or form are required, they can be duplicated or photocopied from a master copy. The method used for this process will depend on several factors, mainly the number of copies, the quality and cost.

Stencil duplicating

Stencils consist of a very thin skin with a plastic coating through which ink will not pass, and a backing sheet. The stencil is the master copy, and is cut by a stencil key on a typewriter with the ribbon out of action and the keys thoroughly cleaned to prevent a smudged outline. If drawings or handwriting has to be reproduced then the stencil can be cut by a 'stylus' pen. It is then placed on to the inked drum of a duplicating machine (Fig. 6.9) and the ink is then forced through the cuts in the stencil and the copy is produced on absorbent paper. Electronic stencil cutting is becoming more popular for, although more expensive than the ordinary method, it is still less expensive than printing.

Figure 6.9   *Stencil duplicator (Roneo Alcatel Ltd)*

Advantages
1. Good quality stencils can produce several hundred copies per run, and, if stored carefully, can be reused.
2. Correction of errors or alterations on the stencil are easily made by using special correcting fluid.
3. Electronic stencils produce photographic reproduction.
4. The absorbent copy paper is reasonably cheap.

Spirit duplicating (Fig. 6.10)

This method of duplicating can reproduce typewriting, handwriting or drawings in a variety of colours. The master copy is made on special coated paper which has a glossy surface on one side. Hectographic carbon paper is placed with its coated surface upwards and the glossy surface of the special paper is placed down on to it. Whatever has to be copied is typed or handwritten on to the exposed surface of the special paper creating a reverse image in carbon on the back of the paper. The master copy is then placed round the drum of the duplicator. The copy paper fed into the machine is automatically dampened with a spirit which will dissolve some of the carbon. It then passes under a roller which presses it against the master copy, leaving a positive image on the copy paper.

Advantages
1. 100–250 copies can be obtained from the master copy or it can be used for short runs until the carbon deposit is exhausted.
2. This is the only method that can reproduce several colours simultaneously by the simple process of writing over different coloured carbon papers in turn when preparing the master copy.
3. Both the carbon and special master paper are reasonably cheap.

Figure 6.10 *Spirit duplicator (Roneo Alcatel Ltd)*

Figure 6.11 *Offset litho duplicator (Roneo Alcatel Ltd)*

Offset lithography (Fig. 6.11)

Lithographic duplicators work on the principle that oil and water do not mix. The master copy is prepared on a thin metal plate or special paper. A specially inked ribbon must be used if it is typed; handwriting or drawings require the use of a special pen. The master is placed on a drum and comes into contact with damp rollers then ink rollers. The blank spaces become wet and therefore reject the printing ink. The greasy impression made by the special typewriter ribbon or special pen rejects the water and takes the ink, and the positive image is 'offset' or transferred to a second roller and is picked up in reverse. When the paper is fed between this second roller and an impression roller, the image is printed the right way round. This is a printing process and a machine would only be practical if the volume of office printing was high.

Advantages
1. Up to 50 000 copies can be obtained from a metal master copy, which can be stored for reuse.
2. High quality reproduction.
3. A cheap form of printing.

Typeset lithography

These duplicators are basically small printing presses and only economic when there is a regular flow of work calling for high quality printing.

Photocopying (Fig. 6.12)

There are many modern photocopying machines on the market. The methods and processes differ but the equipment used consists basically of the original to be photocopied being exposed to light or heat, together with a special light or heat-sensitive paper, and a processing unit in which the copy paper is developed. When many copies of a document are required, photocopying can prove expensive.

Advantages
1. Exact facsimile copies.
2. Simplicity of operation.
3. Useful for making copies of incoming letters, copy invoices, complicated official or legal documents.

Figure 6.12 *Photocopying: The Roneo Rapier 230R Copier (Roneo Alcatel Ltd)*

6.8 THE ELECTRONIC OFFICE

Microcomputer software (program etc.) manufacturers are revolutionising office procedures by producing advanced software systems with facilities that include:

(a) sophisticated word processors;
(b) comprehensive calculators;
(c) communications systems;
(d) flexibility that allows the tailoring of the office specially to the requirements of the establishment.

Filing (Fig. 6.13)

1. The system allows information to be 'filed' on floppy discs so that stored information can be called up at any time on the computer's visual display unit.
2. Records can be updated or deleted.
3. Search can be made through a number of different files at the same time.

Word processors

A word processor is a screen-based memory system which means that if you type a letter or a calculation on the visual display unit then press the print-out command, the letter or calculation will be typed exactly as it is on the screen.

Advantages
1. Standard letters can be stored on floppy discs.
2. If you want to add or remove words from documents the text is adjusted automatically.
3. Calculations for invoices or statement can be used in conjunction with the word-processing facilities.
4. Spelling mistakes can be adjusted or a document redrafted.
5. Letters can be compiled from standard paragraphs stored in the memory.

Accounting

1. All calculations can be carried out by the computer, e.g. discounts, VAT, etc.
2. Calculations can be carried out using information from the files.
3. Results can be printed in any form using the word processor.

Figure 6.13 *Floppy disc trays print-out storage*

6.9   CONTROL SYSTEMS

In the hotel and catering business, as in all other types of business, control should be exercised over all operations throughout the establishment, for control attacks fraud and ineffectiveness and promotes efficiency.

The triplicate checking system (Fig. 6.14) for restaurant control

Under this system a triplicate check pad is used. Each pad has an identifying number, and each check is numbered consecutively. No check should ever be destroyed; if errors are made, the word 'cancelled' should be written across the face and it should be left in its numbered order. The basis of the system as used by the restaurant is as follows:

1.   On each check the waiter or wine waiter must fill in the date, table or room number and details of the order and sign his or her initials or number (Figs. 6.14(b) and (c)).
2.   The *top* copy of the check is handed into the kitchen or bar for the order to be taken. The *second* copy is handed to the cashier who uses it to prepare the customer's bill and the *third* copy is retained in the waiter's book.
3.   The cashier's bills (Fig. 6.14(a)) are made out in duplicate. The top copy acts as a receipt if the customer pays cash, or as a charging source on the tabular ledger for its residents or account customers. Analysis sheets (Fig. 6.15) are written up from the duplicate copies of the bills.
4.   In the control office the top copies of the waiters' checks from the kitchen or bar, together with the second copies from the cashiers, are checked against charged bills, duplicates of the paid bills and summary sheets to ensure that the pricing is correct and that everything has been charged.
5.   Charged bills are sent to the reception office for entry in the tabular ledger. They are then returned to the control office.

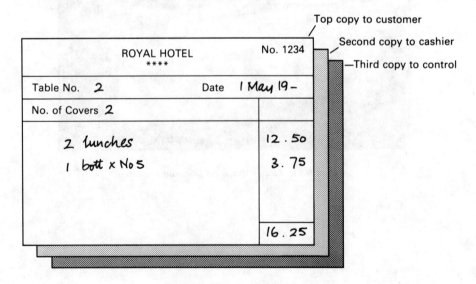

Figure 6.14(a)   *Cashier's bill*

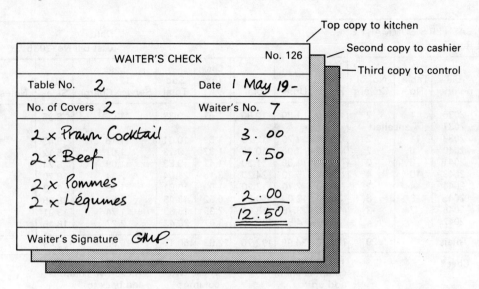

Figure 6.14(b) *Waiter's check*

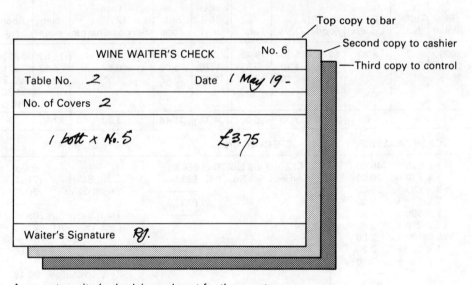

A separate waiter's check is made out for the sweet course

Figure 6.14(c) *Wine waiter's check*

CASHIER'S SUMMARY SHEET
Restaurant

Date
Last Bill No. 2035

Bill number	Table No.	No. of Covers	Food	Drink	Total	Less 15% VAT	Sub Total	Less 12½% Service Charge	Net Sales	Notes
2036	1	2	9.50	1.30	10.80	1.41	9.39	1.04	8.35	
2037	Cancelled									
2038	11	2	9.50	2.70	12.20	1.59	10.61	1.18	9.43	
2040	6	2	9.50	1.00	10.50	1.37	9.13	1.01	8.12	
2041	8	2	9.50	1.80	11.30	1.47	9.83	1.09	8.74	
2043	10	4	19.00	5.20	24.20	3.16	21.04	2.34	18.70	
2044	4	2	9.50	2.70	12.20	1.59	10.61	1.18	9.43	
2045	3	8	38.00	12.00	50.00	6.52	43.48	4.83	38.65	
2046	2	3	14.25	3.75	18.00	2.35	15.65	1.74	13.91	
2047	7	4	19.00	4.50	23.50	3.07	20.43	2.27	18.16	
Totals		29	137.75	34.95	172.70	22.53	150.17	16.68	133.49	

Check — These two columns should add up to / These two columns add back to / These two columns add back to

CREDIT BILLS

Bill number	Table No.	No. of Covers	Food	Drink	Total	Less 15% VAT	Sub Total	Less 12½% Service Charge	Net sales	Room No.
2039	9	3	14.25	5.20	19.45	2.54	16.91	1.88	15.03	302
2042	5	1	4.75	1.10	5.85	0.76	5.09	0.57	4.52	201
2048	12	2	9.50	1.40	10.90	1.42	9.48	1.05	8.43	A/C TO ABC LTD
Total		6	28.50	7.70	36.20	4.72	31.48	3.50	27.98	

CASH ANALYSIS	CHEQUES/Credit Cards	SUMMARY

CASH ANALYSIS

2 × £20 =	40.00
2 × £10 =	20.00
5 × £5 =	25.00
5 × £1 =	5.00
9 × 50p =	4.50
12 × 20p =	2.40
20 × 10p =	2.00
4 × 5p =	0.20
5 × 2p =	0.10
	99.20
	73.50
Cheque & Access	172.70

CHEQUES/Credit Cards

Cheque Bill No. 2045 £50.00
Access Bill No. 2047 £23.50
—
£73.50
—

SUMMARY

	£ p
Cash Sales	172.70
Credit Sales	36.20
Total Sales	208.90
Less 15% VAT	27.25
	181.65
Less 12½% Service charge	20.18
Total Net Sales	161.47

Figure 6.15 *Cashier's summary sheet*

This triple checking system can be used for other items to be charged by the hotel. Books of triplicate checks are issued to the following staff, and in each case, one copy is sent to the control office for checking and another to the reception office as a source for charges on the tabular ledger.

Floor service waiters	Room service
Chambermaids	Early morning teas
Porters	Taxis, newspapers, sundry items
Telephonist	Telephone calls
Barstaff	Drinks
Lounge waiters	Beverages
Garage attendants	Garage
Housekeepers	Laundry and drycleaning

Using colours helps facilitate the sorting of checks and the analysis work done in the control office. Different coloured books of checks can be used for easier identification of the various departments from which the charges originated.

Audit roll control

Checks should be made that the total on the tally roll of all the tills in restaurants, bars, and cash desks should agree with the cash returned by the cashiers. A senior clerk should clear the machines and then reset them to zero at various times during the day.

Cash sales summary

	£
Till reading at end of service:	125.29
Till reading at start of service:	52.40
Total cash paid in:	£72.89

Stock control

It is essential that control should be kept over all stock, whether it be food, drink or items of equipment. A good system for ordering and recording the receipt of all items is necessary and regular stock checks should be made. The basis of a good stock control system is as follows:

1. When goods are received into the stores, cellars, linen rooms or other sections, they are checked against the delivery note and a copy of the order and entered in the goods received book.
2. Goods are binned and entered on the 'bin cards' (Fig. 6.16).
3. The goods received are also posted to the individual stock record cards from the invoice which will show the prices (Fig. 6.17).

Bin card

Item			Maximum stock		
Description/pack size			Minimum stock		
Suppliers			Re-order point		
Price			Other information		
Date	Details		Received in	Booked out	Balance in stock

Figure 6.16 *Bin card*

Stock record card

					Suppliers					
Item										
Description										
Date	Quantity	Details	Unit value		Received in		Booked out		Stock in hand	
			£	P	£	P	£	P	£	P

Figure 6.17 *Stock record card*

4. Departmental requisitions are used to book items out from stores, cellars, linen rooms, etc. (Fig. 6.18).
5. Goods are issued and the requisitions are used to post the times used to the bin cards and stock record cards.
6. Requisitions are used to compile an issue analysis sheet.
7. Regular stock checks should be made to see that the balance of stock in the bin agrees with both the balance on the bin card and the balance on the stock record card.

Requisition			Number		
Tc					
From			Date		
Quantity	Unit	Details	Unit value	£	P
Received by		Authorised by			

Figure 6.18   *Requisition for drawing stock from stores*

6.10 WAGES SYSTEMS

There are many patented wages systems in use especially adapted to meet the requirements of the individual employers, but the basic principles underlying all the systems are the same.

1. To provide records of work and attendance and the pay rates of all members of staff.
2. To calculate the gross pay of each employee, which includes basic pay plus any extra payment in respect of overtime, bonuses, share of service charge, allowances, holiday pay, sick pay and expenses.
3. To calculate the net pay which means subtracting the various deductions from gross pay such as income tax, national insurance contributions, and any other deductions specific to the organisation such as pension contributions, savings clubs and social clubs.
4. To conform to the statutory requirements in respect of the deduction of income tax and national insurance, and the Wages Councils Act 1959.
5. To prepare the payroll and payslips for the employees.

6. To maintain all income tax and national insurance records and keep them up to date.
7. To distribute on time pay envelopes to members of staff.
8. To ensure that income tax and national insurance contributions (including employer's contributions) are paid to the local inspector of taxes.

The payroll

In a large establishment employees are each given a works number, which is entered in numerical order on the weekly payroll sheet or a separate payroll sheet kept for each department. Some hotels use accounting machines which can produce the payroll, tax deduction records and payslips simultaneously. Some patent systems produce a master payroll sheet and a perforated top copy, which can be torn off in strips to provide individual payslips for the employees; details of pay and deductions for each employee are entered on the top copy and appear as a carbon copy on the master sheet. The perforated slips are then torn off and placed in the pay envelopes of the employees.

PAYE (Pay-as-you-earn)

This system means that income tax is deducted from the wages as they are earned. The employer has the responsibility of deducting the income tax from the employee's salary, maintaining all records and sending the tax deducted to the local inspector of taxes. Each worker is given an income tax code number which is related to the total of his personal allowances. His income tax liability is then calculated by referring to tax tables which are supplied by the Inland Revenue.

Example: PAYE

	£
Weekly wages	100
Less Free pay according to personal allowances code No.	48
Taxable pay	£52

Tax tables

Income tax must be deducted or refunded in accordance with these:

Table A — The free pay table
Table B — The taxable pay table

Meal vouchers are not regarded as taxable. *Gratuities* (tips) or a share in a service charge distribution should be included in the gross pay.

Income tax documents

Along with the tax tables, the Inland Revenue issues an *Employer's Guide to PAYE* booklet (P7) which gives instructions on the preparation and use of the official income tax forms and documents.

1. P11 — This is a weekly/monthly tax deduction card, one to be maintained for each employee.

2. P45 — This form is in triplicate and must be handed to all employees leaving a firm. It shows their tax code number and details of their gross pay and tax deducted to date. The top copy is detached and sent to the firm's local tax inspector. Parts II and III are handed to the employees to take to their next employers, who will copy the details on to the P11 card, file Part II for reference and complete Part III and send it to their local inspector of taxes.
3. P46 — This form has to be completed by the employer when a new employee does not produce a P45.
4. P60 — This is a certificate issued to every employee at the end of the financial year showing the amount of gross pay and tax deducted during the year.
5. P35 — At the end of the financial year the employer has to complete this return and send it with the completed P11's to the Collector of Taxes.
6. P47 — Employer's application to the inspector of taxes for authority to refund tax over £20.

National insurance contributions

The Social Security Act 1973, came into operation on 6 April 1975. Earnings-related contributions are collected along with income tax under the pay-as-you-earn system. The following are the rates that were effective from 6 April 1976, but it must be remembered that these are liable to change at any time; full information on contribution rates can be obtained from the Department of Health and Social Security.

Employee's contributions
These contributions are payable at two different rates:
(a) *standard rates* to be paid by most employees;
(b) *reduced rates* payable by certain married women and widows.

Employer's contributions
The contributions paid by employers are at the same rate, regardless of whether the employee pays at standard or reduced rate.

Contribution Rates 1982

Basic scheme	% of gross pay	Employees' contribution	Employer's contribution
Standard rate	14.50%	7.75%	13.7%
Reduced rate	10.75%	2.75%	13.7%

Recording and payment of national insurance contributions
The Department of Health and Social Security allocates national insurance numbers to all contributors and these numbers must be entered on all relevant documents. New employees normally produce a P45 on which their national insurance numbers will have been entered by their previous employers. The P11 tax deduction card provides columns for the recording of the contributions, Col. I(a) for the total of the employee's and employer's contribution, Col. I(b) for the amount of the employee's contribution.

Contribution tables
These tables are produced by the Department of Health and Social Security. They cover earning periods of one week and one month and are used to calculate the contributions to be paid. There are three tables for each set and each bears a distinct category letter which is entered on the P11.

Table A — for standard rate contributions;
Table B — for reduced rate contributions;
Table C — for use where the employee is not liable for any contributions.

End of year procedures
At the end of the financial year the employer must ensure that:
(a) the employee's national insurance number, surname and forenames are correctly entered on every deduction card;
(b) the identifying letter of the contribution table used has been entered on the deduction card and that contribution totals are correct.

The employer's annual declaration (P35)
This annual return made by the employer covers both income tax and national insurance contributions. The total amount of contributions and tax paid by each employee is entered on the P35. All completed deduction cards, the P35 and the balance of any tax or contributions due should be sent to the Collector of Taxes.

Wages Councils Act 1959

In the hotel and catering industry five separate wages boards implement the Wages Councils Act 1959, with regard to the statutory minimum remuneration and holidays and holiday remuneration within the industry. It is likely they may be amalgamated or changed in the future, but at the time of writing they are:

(a) the Industrial and Staff Canteen Undertaking Wages Board (ISC);
(b) the Unlicensed Place of Refreshment Wages Board (UPR);
(c) the Licensed Residential and Licensed Restaurant Wages Board (LR);
(d) the Licensed Non-Residential Establishment Wages Board (LNR);
(e) the Unlicensed Residential Establishment Wages Board (UR).

   In the schedules issued by the Catering Wages Councils to employers in the trade the following terms describe the areas:

Area A — The Metropolitan Police District and City of London
Area B — (a)   In England and Wales, the districts of Birmingham, Bradford, Bristol, Cardiff, Coventry, Kingston-upon-Hull, Leeds, Leicester, Liverpool, Manchester, Newcastle-upon-Tyne, Nottingham, Sheffield and Stoke-on-Trent
            (b)   In Scotland, the Cities of Edinburgh and Glasgow
Area C — All other areas than Area A or B

6.11 PROGRESS TEST QUESTIONS

1. Explain briefly how you would deal with:
   (a) mail for guests in residence;
   (b) mail for departed guests;
   (c) mail for guests yet to arrive.
2. When receiving registered mail for an expected guest, what procedure would you follow?
3. Describe briefly the following methods of despatching outward mail:
   (a) recorded delivery;
   (b) special delivery.
4. Describe the purpose and use of a franking machine.
5. Explain briefly the five basic classifications for filing.
6. Write brief notes on the following methods of reproduction:
   (a) stencil duplicating;   (c) offset lithography;
   (b) spirit duplicating;   (d) photocopying.
7. Explain the triplicate checking system for restaurant control.
8. Describe the basic principles of a good stock control system.
9. Write brief notes on the following terms:
   (a) PAYE;
   (b) Tax Tables A and B;
   (c) P9, P11, P45, P46, P60, P35;
   (d) national insurance contributions Tables A, B and C.
10. Name the five separate wages boards which implement the Wage Councils Act, 1959, in the hotel and catering industry.

7 Reports and statistics

In modern business organisations, reports, statistics, graphs and charts are prepared regularly as an aid to management. They provide information and data which help guide and control the affairs of the business and assist management to make decisions on policy and future developments. Percentages, accounting ratios and averages are helpful in presenting the operational information in a simple manner.

7.1 PERCENTAGES

The simple method of calculating percentages are as follows:

Rule
Multiply quantity by rate and move decimal point two places to left:

Example
What is 6½% of £32.40?

      (rate)   (quantity)

$$32.40$$
$$\times\ 6$$

194.40   6%
16.20   ½% (+ ½ of quantity)

210.60   Move decimal point 2 places to left

Answer £2.106 (£2.11)

Example What percentage is £525 of £1750?

    Method $\dfrac{52500}{1750}$ Add 2 noughts to the top figure and divide by the bottom figure

         = 30%

Example What percentage is £0.77 of £3.50?

    Method $\dfrac{7700}{350} = 22\%$

7.2 ACCOUNTING RATIOS

A ratio is a way of expressing the relationship of one figure to another, for example:

$$\frac{£75\ 000}{£300\ 000} = \text{a ratio of 1:4. Expressed as a percentage:}$$

$$\frac{£75\ 000}{300\ 000} \times \frac{100}{1} = 25\%$$

(£75 000 goes into £300 000 4 times)

$$\frac{£60\ 000}{£15\ 000} = \text{a ratio of 4:1. Expressed as a percentage:}$$

$$\frac{£60\ 000}{£15\ 000} \times \frac{100}{1} = 400\%$$

7.3 AVERAGES

When preparing statistics on guest spending power, room sales and length of stay of guests it is common practice to use averages. There are three methods of arriving at averages:

1. Mean — Add the weekly totals and divide by the number of weeks they cover.
2. Median — Arrange the figures in either ascending or descending order.
    If the number of figures is odd, select the middle figure.
    If the number of figures is even, add the two middle figures together and divide by
    two.
3. Mode — This is the most frequently repeated figure in the series.

MEAN		MEDIAN	MODE
Week No.	Room sales		
	£	£	£
1	3680	3920	3680
2	3760	3840	3760*
3	3720	3760	3720
4	3760	3760	3760*
		—— median	
5	3680	3760	3680
6	3760	3720	3760*
7	3840	3680	3840
8	3920	3680	3920
	Total 8) 30120		
Average	3765	3760	3760

Figure 7.1 *Averages*

The moving average

This method of calculating an average is favoured by the hotel and catering industry as it can show the trend over a period of time and eliminates the effects of seasonal fluctuations.

Method

At the end of each month the top figure is removed and the new month's figure is added and a new average is calculated.

Example

	Sales
	£
January	5 750
February	5 500
March	6 300

$$17\ 550 \div 3 = £5850 \text{ average}$$

	Sales
	£
February	5 500
March	6 300
April	6 700

$$18\ 500 \div 3 = £6167 \text{ average (to nearest £1)}$$

7.4 SALES MIX PERCENTAGES

The term 'sales mix' is used to denote how the total volume of sales is composed and what percentage of that total is contributed by each revenue-producing department.

Example	£	Percentage of sales
Accommodation sales	130 000	52
Restaurant sales	80 000	32
Bar sales	35 000	14
Other sales	5 000	2
Total sales	250 000	100

Method

Accommodation sales $\dfrac{130\ 000}{250\ 000} \times \dfrac{100}{1} = 52\%$

Restaurant sales $\dfrac{80\ 000}{250\ 000} \times \dfrac{100}{1} = 32\%$

Bar sales $\dfrac{35\ 000}{250\ 000} \times \dfrac{100}{1} = 14\%$

Other sales $\dfrac{5\ 000}{250\ 000} \times \dfrac{100}{1} = 2\%$

ROOM OCCUPANCY/BED OCCUPANCY

As the sale of accommodation produces the highest proportion of the income of a hotel, daily occupancy reports are prepared and analysed in order that management can measure whether the hotel is operating to its maximum efficiency.

Room occupancy

To calculate the room occupancy percentage accurately, the number of rooms out of service (OSS) for any reason such as maintenance or redecorating must be deducted from the total number of rooms in the hotel.

Example

Total number of rooms in hotel	200
Less number of rooms OSS	18
Number of rooms available for letting	182

$$\frac{\text{Number of rooms occupied}}{\text{Number of rooms for let}} \quad \frac{135}{182} \times \frac{100}{1} = 74.2\%$$

Room occupancy percentage = 74.2%

Bed occupancy

A more accurate method of measuring the efficiency of the sales department is to calculate the actual bed occupancy (sleepers) percentage.

Example

$$\frac{\text{Number of sleepers}}{\text{Maximum guest capacity}} \quad \frac{245}{324} \times \frac{100}{1} = 75.6\%$$

Bed occupancy percentage = 75.6%

Double occupancy

To measure the skill of the reservations clerk in achieving a maximum occupancy percentage the following calculations can be made.

1. $\dfrac{\text{Number of doubles/twins let as double/twins}}{\text{Number of doubles/twins available}} \quad \dfrac{30}{50} \times \dfrac{100}{1} = 60\%$

2. $\dfrac{\text{Number of doubles/twins let as singles}}{\text{Number of doubles/twins available}} \quad \dfrac{5}{50} \times \dfrac{100}{1} = 10\%$

3. $\dfrac{\text{Number of doubles/twins not let}}{\text{Number of doubles/twins available}} \quad \dfrac{15}{50} \times \dfrac{100}{1} = 30\%$

This type of calculation could reflect the revenue that would be lost by offering a 'middle rate'.

HOUSEKEEPER'S ROOM OCCUPANCY REPORT											
Date 1 June 19--									Time 2200 hrs		
Floor 1				Floor 2				Floor 3			
Room No.	Type	Let ✓	No. of Sleepers	Room No.	Type	Let ✓	No. of Sleepers	Room No.	Type	Let ✓	No. of Sleepers
101	SB	✓	1	201	SB	OOS		301	SB	OOS	
102	SB	✓	1	202	SB	✓	1	302	SB	✓	1
103	SB	✓	1	203	SB	✓	1	303	SB	✓	1
104	SB	✓	1	204	SB	✓	1	304	SB	✓	1
105	TB	✓	2	205	TB			305	TB	OOS	
106	TB	OOS		206	TB			306	TB	✓	1
107	TB	✓	2	207	TB	✓	2	307	TB	OOS	
108	TB	✓	2	208	TB			308	TB		
109	DB	✓	2	209	DB	OOS		309	DB		
110	DB	✓	2	210	DB	✓	2	310	DB		
		9	14			5	7			4	4

Key: SB — Single with Bath	Signature	
TB — Twin with Bath		
DB — Double with Bath	Maximum No. of Rooms for let	24
OOS— Out of Service	Maximum No. of Sleepers	38

ANALYSIS

$$\text{Room occupancy \%} = \frac{\text{No. of Rooms Let}}{\text{Maximum No. of Rooms}} = \frac{18}{24} \times \frac{100}{1} = 75\%$$

$$\text{Bed occupancy \%} = \frac{\text{No. of Sleepers}}{\text{Maximum No. of Sleepers}} = \frac{25}{38} \times \frac{100}{1} = 65.8\%$$

$$\text{Out of Service \%} = \frac{\text{Rooms OOS}}{\text{Maximum No. of Rooms \%}} = \frac{6}{24} \times \frac{100}{1} = 25\%$$

$$\text{Sleeper loss \%} = \frac{\text{No. of Sleepers lost}}{\text{Maximum No. of Sleepers}} = \frac{10}{38} \times \frac{100}{1} = 26.3\%$$

Figure 7.2 *Housekeeper's room occupancy report*

Housekeeper's report (Figs. 7.2 and 7.3)

Each day the housekeeper prepares a room occupancy report and from this the statistics on room occupancy, bed occupancy, rooms out of service and sleeper loss percentages are calculated.

		Total			
Room Type		Rooms	LET	VACANT	OOS
Floor	SB	4	4	—	—
	TB	4	3	—	1
	DB	2	2	—	—
Floor 2	SB	4	3	—	1
	TB	4	1	3	—
	DB	2	1	—	1
Floor 3	SB	4	3	—	1
	TB	4	1	1	2
	DB	2	—	2	—
Total		30	18	6	6

HOUSEKEEPER'S REPORT
Date 1.6.19—— SUMMARY Time 2200 hrs

Analysis

$$\text{LET} \quad \frac{18}{30} = 60\%$$

$$\text{VACANT} \quad \frac{6}{30} = 20\%$$

$$\text{OOS} \quad \frac{6}{30} = 20\%$$

Total Rooms 30 = 100%

Figure 7.3 *Housekeeper's summary report*

7.6 AVERAGE LENGTH OF STAY

To assist the management in organising staff, shifts, holidays and rotas utilising time and equipment a useful statistic is calculating the average length of stay of the guest.

Example
During the course of one week four hundred guests were booked into a hotel. An analysis showed:

In 1982 the statistics showed that in Great Britain:
1. The overall occupancy:
    Average room occupancy 60%
    Average bed occupancy 51%
2. Countryside hotels:
    Average room occupancy 56%
    Average bed occupancy 47%
3. London hotels:
    Average room occupancy 68%
    Average bed occupancy 56%

Length of stay	Number of guests	Sleeper nights
1 night ×	102 =	102
2 nights ×	130 =	260
3 nights ×	80 =	240
4 nights ×	40 =	160
5 nights ×	28 =	140
6 nights ×	10 =	60
7 nights ×	10 =	70
Total	400 =	1032

Average length of stay $= \dfrac{1032}{400} = 2.58$ nights

Figure 7.4

7.7 GRAPHS AND CHARTS

Some hotels maintain graphs and charts to be used for easy visual reference and to gain an overall picture without having to refer to detailed records. The information tabulated is shown as a graph in Fig. 7.5(a) and as a bar chart in Fig. 7.5(b).

No. of rooms: 220   Grand Hotel   Guest capacity: 370

Date	Rooms occupied	Rate of room occupancy %	No. of guests	Rate of bed occupancy %
19—				
15 May	132	60	222	60
15 June	141	64	241	65
15 July	176	80	307	83
15 August	218	99	359	97
15 September	187	85	311	84

7.8 OVERSEAS VISITORS PERCENTAGE

Many hotels maintain records and statistics relating to overseas visitors and their nationality. Tourists from other countries account for a great deal of revenue to some large hotels and therefore a watchful eye is kept on the figure, so that advertising campaigns can be planned to attract foreign visitors.

Example

$$\frac{\text{Total number of overseas visitors}}{\text{Total number of visitors}} \quad \frac{2\ 850}{10\ 200} \times \frac{100}{1} = 27.9\%$$

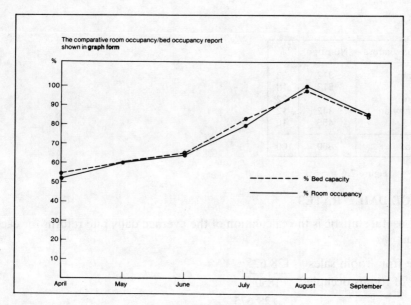

Figure 7.5(a) *The comparative room occupancy/bed occupancy report shown in graph form*

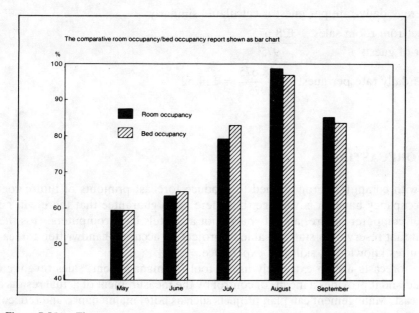

Figure 7.5(b) *The comparative room occupancy/bed occupancy report shown as a bar chart*

Analysis

Overseas visitors	Number	%
American	912	32
French	513	18
German	627	22
Scandinavian	342	12
Others	456	16
Total	2850	100

Figure 7.6

AVERAGE DAILY RATES

Another useful statistic is the calculation of the average daily rate returns for each room occupied:

$$\frac{\text{Revenue from room sales}}{\text{Number of rooms occupied}} \quad \frac{£28\ 675}{1850}$$

$$\text{Average daily rate per room} = \frac{£28\ 675}{1850} = £15.50$$

The average daily rate per guest is calculated similarly:

$$\frac{\text{Revenue from room sales}}{\text{Number of guests}} \quad \frac{£28\ 675}{1975}$$

$$\text{Average daily rate per guest} \quad \frac{£28\ 675}{1975} = £14.52$$

7.10 FORECASTING

Hotels with computers programmed to produce forecast printouts of future room and guest occupancy have an advantage, but there is no guarantee that there will not be a power or computer failure, and of course not all hotels have computers. It is therefore essential that reservation staff are able to project an accurate handwritten forecast, and this requires knowledge, skill and experience.

These forecasts are an extremely useful tool for management; sales revenue can be estimated and it provides a means of control by the measurement of actual results against the forecast. Management can plan projects such as hotel maintenance and redecorating; advertising campaigns can be directed so as to improve low occupancy percentages. Heads of departments can forecast their purchase requirements and plan the labour and holiday rotas.

The forecasts period can cover 7 days, 11 days, 30 days or 90 days, depending entirely on management policy. The information necessary to project the forecast is:

(a)   the actual number of rooms confirmed as shown by the reservations chart of scan;
(b)   a study of the reservations chart for the same period last year;
(c)   a calculation of the average walk-ins or chance guests;
(d)   a calculation of the percentage no shows;

| * * * * **GRAND HOTEL** * * * * |
| **WESTBOURNE** |

Max: Rooms: 297	October 3rd–13th 19—
Max: Guests 415	
Formula: Rooms × 1.40 guests	11 day forecast

	ACTUAL	FORECAST				
DATE	Rooms reserved	Rooms	Guests	Arrivals	Departures	% occupancy
Wednesday 3.10	175	180	252	101	88	60.6
Thursday 4.10	151	170	238	100	110	57.2
Friday 5.10	297	297	415	251	124	100.0
Saturday 6.10	287	297	415	74	74	100.0
Sunday 7.10	68	77	108	50	270	25.9
Monday 8.10	75	108	151	91	60	36.4
Tuesday 9.10	204	242	339	200	66	81.5
Wednesday 10.10	297	297	415	146	91	100.0
Thursday 11.10	297	297	415	139	139	100.0
Friday 12.10	238	297	415	168	168	100.0
Saturday 13.10	154	225	315	71	143	75.8
Totals	2243	2487	3478	1391	1333	76.1

LAST WEEK'S SUMMARY			
Date	Rooms forecast	Rooms actual	% occupancy forecast	% occupancy actual
---	---	---	---	---
Wednesday 26.9	195	199	65.7	67.0
Thursday 27.9	235	258	79.1	86.9
Friday 28.9	193	200	65.0	67.3
Saturday 29.9	194	184	65.3	62.0
Sunday 30.9	119	106	40.1	35.7
Monday 1.10	158	164	53.2	55.2
Tuesday 2.10	154	167	51.9	56.2
Totals	1248	1278	60.0	61.5

Figure 7.7 *A forecast sheet*

(e) a note of any changes between this period last year and now likely to affect the forecast;

(f) The basic formula for the calculation of guest occupancy; that is:

(i) it is simple to calculate one person in a single room, two in a double, but that would not allow for an extra person in a room or for children; therefore an average is calculated thus:

$$\frac{\text{Actual number of guests for period}}{\text{Number of rooms available for letting}} = \frac{214}{102} = 2.10 \text{ guests per room}$$

(ii) a large transient hotel with a high percentage of double rooms, very often occupied by one person only; therefore:

$$\frac{\text{Actual number of guests for that period}}{\text{Number of rooms available for letting}} = \frac{415}{297} = 1.40 \text{ guests per room}$$

Using the second formula follow the forecast chart (Fig. 7.7) for the period Wednesday, 3 October to Saturday, 13 October (11 days).

Key: to percentage calculations:

Wednesday	Forecast rooms	Percentage occupancy
3.10	$\frac{180}{297} \times \frac{100}{1}$ =	60.6
Totals: (11 days × 297)	$\frac{2487}{3267} \times \frac{100}{1}$ =	76.1

7.11 PROGRESS TEST QUESTIONS

1. Calculate the following percentages:
    (a) 7½% of £22;
    (b) 17½% of £108;
    (c) 12% of £22 360;
    (d) 15% of £42 320;
    (e) 22% of £104 500;

2. Calculate the following percentages:
    (a) £15 600 of £120 000;
    (b) 780 of 1200;
    (c) 1428 of 2100;
    (d) 32 of 480;
    (e) 108 of 720.

3. Calculate the following ratios:
    (a) $\dfrac{£22\ 000}{£110\ 000}$
    (b) $\dfrac{£35\ 000}{7\ 500}$

4. Complete the following table:

VERNON HOTEL		
Length of stay	Number of guests	Sleeper nights
1 night	180	
2 nights	120	
3 nights	140	
4 nights	80	
5 nights	160	
6 nights	30	
7 nights	50	
Total		
Average length of stay		

5. Complete the following table:

MEAN			
Week No.	Room Sales	MEDIAN	MODE
	£		
1	2860		
2	2740		
3	2730		
4	2770		
5	2950		
6	2870		
7	2790		
8	2780		
9	2790		
Average			

6. From the following information calculate the room occupancy percentage:

Total number of rooms in hotel 88
Number of rooms out of service 6
Number of rooms occupied 59

7. (a) Complete the following table:

SALES MIX	£	%
Accommodation Sales	172 800	
Restaurant Sales	96 000	
Bar Sales	41 600	
Other Sales	9 600	
Total Sales		

(b) From the completed table prepare a graph and bar chart.

8. Complete the following table:

ATLANTA HOTEL				
Number of rooms: 300		Guest capacity: 520		
Date	Rooms occupied	Rate of room occupancy	Number of guests	Rate of bed occupancy
19––				
20 June	216		364	
20 July	264		452	
20 August	285		478	
20 September	279		484	
20 October	243		416	
20 November	219		374	

9. Complete the following calculations:
    (a) $\dfrac{\text{Total number of overseas visitors}}{\text{Total number of visitors}} = \dfrac{3152}{9850} = \quad \%$

Overseas visitors	Number	%
French	598	
German	536	
Japanese	347	
Scandinavian	284	
American	914	
Others	473	

10. Complete the following table:
    (a) What percentage of the total takings for the period are the total takings for the:
        (i)   lounge bar;
        (ii) cocktail bar;
        (iii) restaurant;
        (iv) snack bar.
    (b) Calculate the average takings per week for the restaurant over the period.
    (c) If the food cost for the restaurant during the period amounts to £6619.60 calculate:
        (i) the gross profit in monetary terms;
        (ii) the gross profit as a percentage of sales.
    (d) How many snacks at an average cost of 65p each were served during the July period?
    (e) What is the average spending power per customer in the restaurant if 3220 customers were served during the period?

Week ending	Lounge bar £ p	Cocktail bar £ p	Restaurant £ p	Snack bar £ p	Total £ p
3.6.78	240.20	232.10	1275.60	250.30	
10.6.78	243.40	225.10	1282.40	233.10	
17.6.78	226.40	220.20	1296.40	242.10	
24.6.78	236.40	226.40	1302.60	226.00	
TOTAL					
1.7.78	248.60	236.10	1277.30	246.20	
8.7.78	252.50	232.20	1250.40	238.20	
15.7.78	234.40	244.10	1256.20	224.10	
22.7.78	244.20	228.20	1278.60	236.80	
29.7.78	258.40	236.10	1246.20	232.30	
TOTAL					
5.8.78	232.70	222.30	1266.80	240.50	
12.8.78	220.80	230.10	1287.60	231.20	
19.8.78	242.60	240.00	1252.40	239.30	
26.8.78	244.00	243.10	1268.40	227.10	
TOTAL					
TOTALS					

(f) If the purchases for the lounge bar for the period amounts to £1406.07, calculate:
 (i) the gross profit in monetary terms;
 (ii) the gross profit as a percentage of sales.
(g) What percentage of the total takings for August were the takings in the cocktail bar?
11. (a) You are asked to project a eleven-day room occupancy forecast for your hotel; what information would you require in order to proceed?
 (b) Discuss: forecasts as a tool and aid for management, their uses and advantages.

8 Legal aspects

By Alan Pannett

This chapter provides an outline of the law as it relates to the work of a hotel receptionist.

8.1 BOOKING CONTRACTS

A booking contract between a guest and a hotel may come into being in any one of a number of ways. All bookings are made through the receptionist of the hotel.

Normally prospective guests either write or telephone the hotel prior to booking. A booking contract may be formed by a telephone conversation between the prospective guest and the hotel. Only where the words used are sufficient to amount to an offer by one party to the other to contract and an acceptance by that other party of the terms of the offer, will a contract be brought about. It is normal practice for hotels to require confirmation from a prospective guest in writing.

The guest's letter requesting accommodation amounts to an offer to contract; the hotel's written acknowledgement is the acceptance of it. Where bookings occur by an exchange of letters, the initial inquiry by the guest does not amount to an offer to contract, nor necessarily does the hotel's reply to the guest stating the tariff and room availability. It is afterwards when the prospective guest writes to the hotel that he or she requires a room between certain dates that an offer is made. The hotel's response in writing confirming the booking is an acceptance of the guest's offer to contract. The contract is then completely formed. Bookings may also be made as a result of a chance call at reception of the hotel by a person seeking a room. In this situation the traveller's request for a room is merely pre-contractual, the receptionist by telling the traveller that a room is available at a given price for one or more nights is making an offer to the traveller.

The traveller may thereafter accept the terms of the offer, or reject them and seek accommodation elsewhere.

In modern sophisticated hotels bookings may be made by telex. Telex is treated in law as an instant form of communication. Hence, the same principles apply to telex as apply to chance call bookings made on a face-to-face basis.

A hotel receptionist should be sure that prospective guests are aged 18 or more, since otherwise if the bill remains unpaid a court action if brought to recover the debt will fail because the contract of booking is unenforceable.

What are the terms normally included in a contract of booking? The terms of a contract are normally express (i.e. stated by the parties to be part of it). The express terms contained in a booking contract are likely to relate to the following points:

(a) payment and confirmation of booking;
(b) cancellation by either client or hotel;
(c) alteration to the terms of the contract by the hotel;
(d) liability of the hotel for guest's property etc.;
(e) liability of the hotel for unforeseen occurrences.

Terms may not be added to a contract once it has been made. The terms of a contract are settled either before or at the time of making the contract. In *Olley* v. *Marlborough Court Ltd* (1949) the guest booked a room in a hotel. The contract was made at the reception desk. A notice in the guest's room sought to exclude liability for loss or damage to guest's property. A thief gained entry to the guest's room and stole her property. The hotel tried to rely upon the notice in guest's room as excluding their liability for the loss.

The court took the view that since the contract was formed at the reception desk, the notice in the bedroom did not form part of the contract, thus it could not be relied upon by the hotel as excluding liability.

A booking contract will normally come to an end in any of three ways:

(a) performance;
(b) frustration;
(c) breach.

A contract ends by performance when the terms of the contract have been performed by both parties, i.e. the hotelier has supplied the accommodation contracted for and the guest has paid the contract price for the accommodation services rendered.

Frustration is where a contract is terminated by an event which has arisen through no fault of either contracting party. The most likely way in which a booking contract may be frustrated is through severe illness on the part of the guest. Other circumstances which may amount to frustration of a booking contract are the flooding of the hotel so as to make it uninhabitable or its destruction by fire.

Breach of contract occurs where one of the parties fails to perform any one of the contract terms. The effect of the breach will depend upon the nature of the terms breached , if the term breached is a condition, i.e. a fundamental term of the contract, the victim of the breach may treat the contract as at an end and sue for damages. Where the term breached is a less important term, a warranty, breach merely entitles the victim of it to sue for damages and does not allow the victim to end the contract.

In the area of booking contracts a form of damages has developed which may enable the guest to obtain more than the value of the contract. This form of damage is called damages for disappointment. This principle has been extended so that a person who books a holiday on behalf of others, e.g. a husband booking on behalf of himself his wife and children, may obtain damages not only for his own disappointment etc. but also for the disappointment sustained by his wife and children.

What happens where an untrue statement is made which induces a guest to book at the hotel? This does not amount to a breach of contract by the hotel unless the misrepresentaton is incorporated into the contract and thus forms one of its terms. However, where a person is induced to make a contract by a false statement this may give rise to a civil action brought by the party to whom the statement was addressed for misrepresentation under the Misrepresentation Act 1967. In addition, the making of false statements (whether in adverts or otherwise) which are made either knowingly or recklessly may give rise to a criminal prosecution under section 14(1) Trade Descriptions

Act 1968. Such prosecutions are brought by trading standards officers working for the local authority, the purpose of such prosecutions is to punish offenders.

The provisions contained in s.14(1) affect the hotelier in many ways.

Examples
A hotel advertises that the hotel is RAC- and AA- recommended when it is not, this is an offence within the scope of s.14(1). A hotel advertises that it is 100 yards from the beach and all rooms have a sea view. The hotel is half a mile from the beach and none of the rooms overlook the sea. Section 14(1) also applies here. A receptionist assures a potential guest that she has been allocated a room with a bathroom/w.c. and a balcony, when the room in fact allocated has none of these facilities; s.14(1) also applies to this situation.

If a hotel receptionist double-books a room does this give rise to criminal liability? You may be surprised to learn that it can do. The principles of law involved are discussed in section 8.3 of this chapter.

8.2 PRICE DISPLAY

The Tourism (Sleeping Accommodation Price Display) Order 1977 requires the display of overnight accommodation prices in residential establishments with more than four rooms. The notice required by the Order must be clearly displayed either at the entrance to the hotel or at reception. The information which must be provided in the notice comprises:

(a)   price of a single room;
(b)   price of a double room;
(c)   price of any other type of bedroom (e.g. suite);
(d)   all prices must be inclusive of service charge and state this to be so;
(e)   the VAT element in the price must be shown in some form or other;
(f)   it should be made clear whether the stated price is inclusive of meals.

A failure to display such a notice may lead to a criminal prosecution brought by the trading standards office of the local authority. The maximum fine upon convictions for breach of the order is £200. A sample notice is set out below.

TOURISM (SLEEPING ACCOMMODATION PRICE DISPLAY) ORDER 1977

NOTICE

HOTEL NAUTICAL TARIFF

SINGLE ROOM
£20.00 per night plus VAT   (£23.00 total)

DOUBLE ROOM
£35.00 per night plus VAT   (£40.25 total)

CAPTAIN'S SUITE
£50.00 per night plus VAT   (£57.50 total)

All prices include full English breakfast and service charge.

8.3   REGISTERING GUESTS AND OVERBOOKING

Registration of Guests

By virtue of the Immigration (Hotel Records) Order 1972 all guests over the age of sixteen are required upon arrival at a hotel to register their full name and nationality, or have it registered for them. The hotelier is required to keep a record of this information which is open to inspection by the police for a period of up to twelve months.

British subjects and Commonwealth citizens need not give their address. Each guest must be the subject of a separate entry in the hotel register. Non-British and non-Commonwealth citizens must give the following information:

(a)   their name and nationality;
(b)   passport details;
(c)   the date on which they intend to leave and their next destination.

Overbooking

It is a common practice within the hotel industry for hotel reception staff to overbook the rooms available at the hotel to a limited degree in the expectation that certain of the bookings made will be cancelled, 'no shows' as they are sometimes called. The reception staff therefore take a calculated risk that there will be a percentage of 'no shows' and overbook the same percentage of rooms in an effort to maintain full occupancy of the rooms. However, overbooking is an illegal practice following the decision of the House of Lords in *British Airways* v. *Taylor* (1976).

Example
Ms Jones, the hotel receptionist at the Hotel Bograte, overbooks the rooms available at the hotel on the night of 1 April. Ms Jones, in answer to Mr Snoops letter requesting accommodation in room 214 for the night of 1 April, writes confirming the reservation of that particular room.

Mr Snoops arrives at the Hotel Bograte on 1 April and demands to stay in room 214, which has already been let for the night to Mr and Mrs Bunn. Mr Snoop may bring a civil action claiming damages for breach of the booking contract between himself and the Hotel Bograte, including damages for disappointment (see section 8.1 above). Furthermore, provided Ms Jones's original statement reserving room 214 was made either knowingly or recklessly an offence under s.14 Trade Descriptions Act 1968 has been committed. Can the hotel receptionist be prosecuted for an offence under s.14 Trade Descriptions Act 1968? Yes, she or he may be prosecuted. The purpose of the legislation is, however, not to punish individuals, but to promote good business practices and to prevent unconscionable ones. A receptionist will not normally overbook unless it is done in compliance with the policy of the management of the hotel, or upon the instructions of the reception manager. In either case sections 23 and 24 Trade Descriptions Act 1968 allow for the prosecution of the hotel (whether it be a company or a proprietor) or another person who is directly responsible for the commission of the offence, i.e. the reception manager. Section 24 may also be used by a hotelier who is prosecuted under s.14 where the overbooking was due to the actions or default of the receptionist or reception manager and was not part of the hotelier's policy.

8.4 INNS AND HOTELS: THE RIGHTS AND DUTIES OF THE PROPRIETOR

When looking at booking contracts above we did not distinguish between the various forms of establishment which offer food, drink and accommodation. The law of England does in fact draw a distinction between 'inns' and other establishments. The term 'inn' is given a technical meaning: it describes those hotels which fall within the scope of the Hotel Proprietors Act 1956. Inn, therefore, has a specific legal meaning and only those establishments which fall within that definition are subject to the duties and able to exercise the rights accorded to establishments of that status. The definition of an inn is to be found in s.1(3) of the HPA 1956 — 'an establishment held out by the proprietor as offering food, drink and, if so required, sleeping accommodation, without special contract, to any traveller presenting himself who appears able and willing to pay a reasonable sum for the services and facilities provided and who is in a fit state to be received'.

It is not easy to define in any positive way the kinds of hotel within the scope of s.(3) HPA 1956, but obviously the larger establishments such as major hotels are covered by s.1(3), as are many more modest hotels.

What are the duties which the law imposes upon an innkeeper? The proprietor of an inn is known as an innkeeper, and it is upon this person that the duties arising both at common law and under the Hotel Proprietors Act 1956 are imposed. Such duties are owed by an innkeeper to any traveller calling at the inn. A traveller is any person who calls at the inn to use the services there available. The duties owed to a traveller are:

1. A duty to provide reasonable refreshment. A failure to fulfill this duty on the part of the innkeeper may render the innkeeper liable to criminal prosecution. An innkeeper is however, only bound to supply that which he has available and is not under any duty to send out for further supplies in order to satisfy the traveller's request.
2. A duty to provide accommodation at the inn without prior contract to any traveller seeking accommodation.

    An innkeeper may refuse to accommodate a traveller only when:
    (a) the inn is full;
    (b) the traveller is unable to pay a reasonable sum for the accommodation in advance;
    (c) the traveller is not in a fit state to be received at the inn.

Where the inn is full there is no duty to accommodate. The stranded motorist is a classic example; there is no duty to accommodate stranded travellers when the inn is full. Often innkeepers will make exceptional arrangements for such persons as a gesture of goodwill (e.g. letting them sleep in the lounge), but they cannot legally be required to do so.

When can service be refused to a traveller? The Hotel Proprietors Act 1956 contains two provisos.

1. An innkeeper is not bound to supply with reasonable refreshment or to accommodate, any person who cannot pay a reasonable sum for these services. Reception staff at hotels are often instructed that where they feel cautious about a prospective guest's ability to pay the final bill, payment shall be requested in advance. This is a normal practice where, for instance, the night porter books in a guest after reception has closed. It is a precaution against the guest's departing early the following morning without paying the bill.

2.   An innkeeper can refuse service to any person who is not in a fit state to be received at the inn. An example may be a traveller who has on previous occasions caused annoyance to other guests or in some way disrupted the inn. It is generally appreciated within the hotel industry that this second proviso provides the innkeeper with a broad power to regulate the clientele at the inn. An innkeeper may insist that male customers wear a jacket and tie, refusing to serve persons who are casually dressed. It is also useful when dealing with undesirable customers, e.g. drunks, and prostitutes. Reception staff at hotels based in cities and large towns may have to persuade unwanted persons loitering in the reception lounge to move on and leave the hotel; the right to refuse service to persons unfit to be received is often the authority relied on when taking such actions.

An innkeeper must be careful however, not to refuse service for the wrong reasons. Innkeepers who either discriminate against or refuse service to a customer on the grounds of his or her sex or race are liable to have a claim brought against them under either s.29 of the Sex Discrimination Act 1975 or s.20 of the Race Relations Act 1976. The law regarding discrimination either upon grounds of race or sex is applicable to all establishments irrespective of whether or not the establishment is within the scope of the HPA 1956.

8.5   THE GUEST IN RESIDENCE

Innkeepers' liability for guest's property

Innkeepers have a strict duty to care for the property of their guests. This duty of an innkeeper is owed not to travellers but only to guests; a guest is a person who has engaged a minimum of one night's accommodation at the inn. The innkeeper's liability for guest's property is strict. It does not depend upon proof of neglect on the part of the innkeeper. It is the innkeeper's duty to keep the guest's property safe; the innkeeper's liability is not dependent upon how the goods are lost or damaged. However, loss or damage due to the fault of the guest is not within the scope of the innkeeper's liability. Section 2 of the HPA 1956 sets out the scope of the duty and restricts the kinds of property to which the duty applies. It does not apply to the guest's vehicle or any of the guest's property left in the guest's vehicle.

In order that an innkeeper be strictly liable for loss or damage to the property of a guest, the guest must prove:
(a)   that he or she has been signed in at the inn;
(b)   that at the time of the loss or damage he or she had taken a room at the inn; and
(c)   that the property in question was of a sort covered by the innkeeper's duty.
The scope of the innkeeper's duty is further limited by s.2(3):

> where the proprietor of an hotel is liable as an innkeeper to make good the loss of or damage to property brought to the hotel, his liability to any one guest shall not exceed fifty pounds in respect of any one article, or one hundred pounds in the aggregate, except where —
> (a)   the property was stolen, lost or damaged through the default, neglect or wilful act of the proprietor or some servant of his or
> (b)   the property was deposited by or on behalf of the guest expressly for safe custody with the proprietor or some servant of his authorised, or appearing to be authorised, for the purpose, and, if so required by the proprietor or that servant, in a container fastened or sealed by the depositor; or

(c)   at a time after the guest has arrived at the hotel, either the property in question was offered for deposit as aforesaid and the proprietor or his servant refused to receive it, or the guest or some other guest acting on his behalf wished so to offer the property in question but, through the default of the proprietor or a servant of his, was unable to do so.

Provided that the proprietor shall not be entitled to the protection of this subsection unless, at the time when the property in question was brought to the hotel, a copy of the notice set out in the schedule to this Act printed in plain type was conspicuously displayed in a place where it could conveniently be read by his guests at or near the reception office or desk or, where there is no reception office or desk, at or near the main entrance to the hotel.

The Schedule notice referred to in s.2(3) is set out below.

Schedule to the Hotel Proprietors Act 1956

NOTICE

LOSS OF OR DAMAGE TO GUESTS' PROPERTY

Under the Hotel Proprietors Act 1956, a hotel proprietor may in certain circumstances be liable to make good any loss of or damage to a guest's property even though it was not due to any fault of the proprietor or staff of the hotel.

This liability, however:

(a)   extends only to the property of guests who have engaged sleeping accommodation at the hotel;
(b)   is limited to £50 for any one article and a total of £100 in the case of any one guest, except in the case of property which has been deposited or offered for deposit for safe custody;
(c)   does not cover motor-cars or other vehicles of any kind or any property left in them, or horses or other live animals.

This notice does not constitute an admission either that the Act applies to this hotel or that liability thereunder attaches to the proprietor of this hotel in any particular case.

The effect of s.2(3) of the HPA 1956 is to afford protection to an innkeeper. Provided the innkeeper displays the Schedule notice in the manner stipulated, his liability for loss or damage to any one article of the guest's property is £50. In any event the total liability of the innkeeper for two or more articles of the guest's property cannot exceed £100. Where, however, the loss or damage is due to any of the three matters stipulated in s.2(3)(a), (b), or (c), the innkeeper loses protection and is liable to the guest for the full extent of the loss. On the other hand if the loss or damage to the guest's property is attributable to the misconduct or negligence of the guest, no liability attaches to the innkeeper for the loss or damage.

From the point of view of the hotel receptionist it is important to remember a vital practical point: do not refuse to take guest's property into safe custody, and make sure that either you or one of your staff constantly remain at the reception desk in order to fulfil this duty. A refusal or a failure in this respect may lead to the innkeeper (your employer) being fully liable for those articles tendered for safe custody by reason of s.2(3)(b) and 2(3)(c). Furthermore, always ensure that the Schedule notice is displayed.

A failure to display this notice will mean that the protection afforded by s.2 cannot be utilised if required.

It is possible, and indeed it is the normal practice for innkeepers to insure themselves against the risk of loss or damage to guests' property, thus limiting the likely effect of such an occurrence.

8.6 THE RIGHTS OF AN INNKEEPER

Because innkeepers are under specific duties imposed upon them by the Hotel Proprietors Act 1956 and at common law, they in return have certain rights which they may exercise over and above those which proprietors who are not innkeepers may exercise.

The most important right is the right of lien over guests' property. The term 'lien' merely describes a right exerciseable by one party over the property of another. An innkeeper may detain any property brought to the inn by a guest until the guest has paid his or her bill in full. The innkeeper is not however, entitled to detain the guest. The innkeeper's lien applies both to travellers' and guests' property. An innkeeper, as we have seen, is under a duty to provide reasonable refreshment if so required and accommodation to a traveller; hence, the innkeeper has a right of lien over a traveller's property as well as over a guests' to ensure that the traveller's bill is duly paid. It is unlikely, however, that a traveller will bring luggage to the inn, and since the traveller's car and goods contained therein cannot be the subject of a lien, cases where the lien is exercised over the property of a traveller are rare.

Where an innkeeper exercises the right of lien over the property of a guest, the innkeeper owes to the guest whose property the innkeeper is retaining a duty to take reasonable care of the property in question.

An innkeeper has a power of sale in relation to the goods over which he or she is exercising his or her right of lien. If innkeepers did not have a right of sale they would be left with the property of guests which they could not realise in order to satisfy the debt. The right of sale is subject to certain restrictions as provided by s.1 of the Innkeepers Act 1878.

A table showing the respective rights and duties of an innkeeper compared with those of a proprietor of a private hotel is set out below:

Duties owed by both inns and private hotels.
1. The duty owed as an occupier of premises towards lawful visitors (e.g. guests and travellers) to the premises, under the Occupiers' Liability Act 1957.
2. A civil duty to take reasonable care of guests' property brought to the premises, under the tort of negligence, or as an implied term of the contract of booking.
3. The duty not to discriminate in the provision of services to the public, either on the basis of a person's race or sex — s.20 Race Relations Act 1974, s.29 Sex Discrimination Act 1975.

The rights common to both an innkeeper and the proprietor of a private hotel.
1. The right to control the premises and refuse service so as to maintain good order and decency.

The sole rights of the proprietor of a private hotel.
1.   The right to pick and choose between persons requesting service.
2.   The right to refuse service (subject to statutory restraints as to race and sex discrimination) to any person at the will of the proprietor.

The sole rights of the innkeeper.
1.   The right to demand payment in advance of service.
2.   The innkeeper's lien over property.

The sole duties of the innkeeper.
1.   The duty to provide a traveller with refreshment and, if so required, accommodation.
2.   The strict duty of responsibility for the property of guests at the inn.

8.7   NON-PAYMENT BY GUESTS AND TRAVELLERS

Defaulting is a problem for many forms of catering enterprise. The customer who walks out without paying in a restaurant and the guest at a hotel who leaves early in the morning by a fire escape are but two examples of the problems hoteliers face. Where travellers are provided with food and drink and fail to pay before they depart from the premises, they may be charged with a criminal offence (making off without payment) contrary to s.3(1) of the Theft Act 1978. An innkeeper may demand payment prior to the provision of the service, e.g. food, drink or accommodation; this in itself affords some protection from defaulters.

What should a hotel receptionist do if he or she believes a guest to be dishonest? If the situation is one where the person in question is seeking accommodation, the receptionist may ask the prospective guest to pay for the accommodation, in advance. Innkeepers have a legal right to payment in advance. If the prospective guest is unable to pay then the receptionist may refuse to accommodate that person. If the situation is one where the receptionist believes that the guest may try to leave without paying, the receptionist will normally advise the proprietor of his or her fears and the decision will then be the proprietor's. If the situation requires quick action, there being no time to seek higher authority, the receptionist at an inn may detain the guest's luggage (not the guest himself or his vehicle) and exercise the innkeeper's lien over the guest's property until the bill is paid in full. Both of these examples rely on the rights of an innkeeper which we have considered above; it is of course perfectly proper for the receptionist to call the police as an alternative measure.

8.8   THE HOTEL PREMISES

There are many legal aspects which relate to the hotel premises. An outline is given below of important legal controls on hotel premises.

Hygiene

The Food and Drugs Act 1955, and the Food Hygiene (General) Regulations 1970 control the cleanliness of all establishments concerned with food preparation, hotel kitchens must comply with these regulations. Prosecution for offences under either the 1955 Act or the 1970 Regulations may lead to heavy penalties, and even to the enforced closure of the premises by the Food & Drugs (Control of Food Premises) Act 1976.

Fire

Fire, should it occur in a place where a substantial number of people gather, i.e. a bar or a hotel, may have tragic consequences. These are heightened in a hotel, since many people sleep within one building. The Fire Precautions Act 1971 was passed in order to improve fire safety standards at premises frequented by the general public. Fire certificates are required for certain kinds of premises, including many hotels. These certificates are issued by the local fire authority. An inspection of the premises is carried out and a certificate is only issued where the local fire authority are satisfied that adequate precautions have been taken.

Working conditions

Working conditions are regulated by two major Acts of Parliament, the Offices, Shops and Railway Premises Act 1963, and the Health and Safety at Work etc. Act 1974.

Offices, Shops and Railway Premises Act 1963

The Act applies to office premises, shop premises and railway premises where persons are employed under a contract of employment. Certain premises are excluded from the Act, e.g. small family businesses where only the immediate family are employed. Hence, a small family guest house or tea rooms may be excluded from the Act's operation. The term 'shop premises' covers a number of different premises, including premises from which retail trade or business is carried on. Hence, the Act would appear to cover restaurants, wine bars, etc.

All premises within the scope of the 1963 Act are required to be kept in a clean state. This covers all furniture and fittings, etc. on the premises. Neither dirt nor refuse must be allowed to accumulate, and all floors and stairs shall be cleaned at least once a week. The 1963 Act is directed towards the protection of the workforce rather than the consumer. The 1963 Act also relates to the facilities available at premises covered by the Act, e.g. sanitary conveniences, washing facilities, drinking water and seating facilities for staff.

Some of the provisions of the 1963 Act relate to the structure of the building, that all floors, stairs, steps, passages and gangways shall be of sound construction and properly maintained. Breach of the requirements set out in the 1963 Act is a criminal offence and may lead to prosecution.

Health and Safety at Work etc. Act 1974

This Act is of much broader application than the 1963 Act discussed above. The HSWA 1974 applies to all places where persons are employed, and makes provision for the health and safety of such employees. Employers have a general duty imposed by s.2 of the 1974 Act to safeguard in so far as is reasonably practicable the health, safety and welfare of their employees. Employees should also be given adequate training in safety precautions etc. Employees are themselves under a duty to take reasonable care not to injure others in the course of their work. The 1974 Act is enforced by the Health and Safety Inspectorate, who have various powers, prohibition notices, etc. The Health and Safety Inspectorate may ultimately prosecute the party concerned in the courts, and where a person is found guilty, substantial fines may be imposed.

8.9   LICENSING

The many rules and regulations concerning licensing will only be touched on in this section; they form in themselves a considerable volume of law. The Licensing Act 1964 brought together the earlier liquor licensing legislation. Licences normally take either of two forms: a full on-licence, or an off-licence. A full on-licence enables the licensee to sell liquor for consumption either on or off the premises to any member of the public who is permitted by the law to consume it. An off-licence permits the sale of liquor for consumption off the premises. A hotel may apply for a full on-licence; on the other hand small establishments may merely have a restaurant licence or a residential licence. Where the licensing justices grant a restaurant licence they must attach two conditions:

(a)   the restaurant must be able to serve both water and soft drinks as well as alcohol; and
(b)   alcohol can only be served to persons taking table meals.

A residential licence authorises the sale of liquor to residents of a hotel. Two conditions are attached to the grant of a residential licence:

(a)   other beverages (including water) must be available with meals; and
(b)   adequate seating must be provided in a room at the hotel which is not used as sleeping accommodation or for the service of food, and in which there is neither supply or consumption of intoxicating liquor.

It is possible to combine a residential licence with a restaurant licence.

Permitted hours

It is a criminal offence for any person to sell or supply intoxicating liquor, on licensed premises except during permitted hours. Section 60 of the Licensing Act 1964 lays down the basic permitted laws for on-licences:

Weekdays (excluding Christmas day and Good Friday) 11 a.m. to 3 p.m.
                                                   5.30 p.m. to 11 p.m.
Sundays, Christmas day, Good Friday   Noon to 2 p.m.
                                                   7 p.m. to 10.30 p.m.

Although the basic permitted hours are set there are a number of ways in which these may be varied.

Supper hours certificate
The effect of this is to allow liquor to be provided for a further hour in the evening in a part of the premises set aside for people taking table meals provided it is consumed as part of the meal.

Special hours certificate

This form of extension exists for the benefit of restaurants, hotels etc. where the sale of liquor accompanies the service of refreshment, and music and dancing is provided.

Drinking-up time

After the end of the hours during which sales are permitted, ten minutes is allowed for drinking up liquor already purchased. The drinking-up time is half an hour for people taking meals if the liquor was supplied ancillary to meals. The permitted hours provisions do not apply to any persons in premises where they are residing or to the supply of liquor to private friends of residents in a licensed premises entertained by the residents at their own expense.

The conduct of licensed premises

There are many requirements to be met in order to conduct licensed premises within the scope of the law:

1. Selling liquor without a licence. No licensee may sell liquor without a licence; to do so is a criminal offence.
2. The sale of liquor on credit. It is a criminal offence to sell liquor on credit. However, residents at a hotel may be sold liquor during their residence, payment to be made at the end of their stay.
3. The sale of liquor to persons under 18. A licensee of licensed premises is not permitted knowingly to sell liquor to a person under 18, to allow a person under 18 to consume liquor in a bar, or to allow anyone else to make such a sale. A person who is under 18 is not permitted to buy liquor in licensed premises nor to consume liquor in a bar. No person is allowed to buy liquor for consumption in a bar in licensed premises for a person under 18.
4. Drunkenness and disorderly behaviour. It is an offence to permit drunkenness on licensed premises. Where the licensee holds a residential or restaurant licence it can lead to disqualification of the licensee.

Other forms of licence

There are a number of different forms of entertainment where a licence of some sort or other is required by law. These include gaming, music and dancing.

8.10 PROGRESS TEST QUESTIONS

1. How may a contract of booking come into being?
2. Of what significance is a guest's capacity to contract?
3. How may a contract of booking end?
4. Of what significance is s.14(1) of the Trade Descriptions Act 1968?
5. Examine the possible legal outcome of overbooking.
6. Analyse the definition of an inn under the Hotel Proprietors Act 1956.
7. Of what importance are the innkeeper's duties to provide reasonable refreshment and accommodation to travellers?

8. Of what significance is s.2(3) of the Hotel Proprietors Act 1956?
9. Outline the innkeeper's right of lien and examine its significance and usage.
10. Of what significance are:
    (a)   Fire Precautions Act 1971;
    (b)   Offices, Shops and Railway Premises Act 1963;
    (c)   Health and Safety at Work etc. Act 1974.
11. Outline the legal aspects relating to lost property found on the hotel premises.
12. Write a brief note explaining the meaning of each of the following justices' licenses:
    (a)   on-licence;
    (b)   restaurant licence;
    (c)   residential licence.

9 Ancillary duties, first aid and safety precautions

9.1 ANCILLARY DUTIES

As the communication centre of the hotel, the reception office has to work in close co-operation with all other departments in order that the work of its own section can be carried out efficiently and effectively. Therefore, the receptionist must be aware of the function and organisation of all areas of work in the hotel and of the systems and methods used in each department.

The housekeeping department

One of the busiest executives in the hotel is the head housekeeper, who has the responsibility for the cleanliness and good order of all the bedrooms, bathrooms, corridors, public rooms and offices. The number of staff under the head housekeeper's direction will depend on the size of the hotel, but they will include assistant housekeepers, chambermaids, staff, corridor and bathroom maids and cleaners.

The departmental copy of the arrivals and departures list prepared daily by the reception office is used by the head housekeeper and his or her assistants for informing the staff which rooms have to be cleaned and prepared for new arrivals. Daily duty rotas are prepared allocating the everday tasks to each member of the staff. Rooms must be cleaned and dusted, beds stripped and re-made with clean sheets and pillowcases, and the towels changed. Cleaners are responsible for cleaning, vacuuming and dusting the public rooms, but in some hotels the uniformed staff will do this duty early in the morning before guests get up.

Bed occupancy and room availability reports

It is the head housekeeper's responsibility to check the state of all rooms and to see that all the work allocated to the staff is carried out. Daily reports have to be made on the occupancy of all rooms. These are called 'sleeper' or 'bed occupancy' lists. These lists can be used as a check against the reception records of lettings. Another daily, and, if necessary, twice daily, report has to be made on the rooms that have been cleaned, prepared and are available for letting (Fig. 9.1). This has to be handed into the reception office in order that they have up-to-the-minute information on rooms available and can sell the accommodation effectively.

In very large hotels electronic reception boards are installed which are connected with the housekeeping department, and various coloured lights on the board will indicate the readiness of a room for letting.

Housekeeper's room vacancy report

To: **Reception office**				Date 2nd June, 197..		
The following rooms were vacant at			2 .00 a.m./p.m.	and are ready for letting		

Floor 1	Floor 2	Floor 3	Floor 4	Floor 5		
105˙	201	303	401	Floor being		
110	202	304	402	redecorated		
	203	305	405			
	206	308	407			
	207	309	409			
	208	310	410			

This report must be completed and handed into the Reception office daily

at 10.00 a.m.
2.00 p.m.
7.00 p.m.   Signature   *A. Jones*

Figure 9.1   *Housekeeper's room vacancy report*

The linen room

The head housekeeper usually supervises and controls the linen room, but in large hotels a linenkeeper is employed solely to maintain and care for all the sheets, pillowcases, blankets, towels, tablecloths, napkins and other sundry items which are used daily. All linen must be kept in good repair and no soiled or torn linen must be issued. Stock records must be maintained and when linen is sent to the laundry it should be counted and checked, and when it is returned by the laundry it should be counted and checked again. In normal circumstances fresh linen is only issued on the receipt of dirty linen from each bedroom. Any special requests such as extra pillows, blankets or cots to be placed in bedrooms are notified to the head housekeeper who will draw the necessary linen from stock. (If the reception office receives any such requests on their booking forms, they will notify the head housekeeper on an internal memorandum form.)

Tablecloths, napkins and other sundry items used by the restaurants may or may not be kept in a separate linen room, but the procedure is still the same — the issue of clean linen to the restaurant is usually on receipt of a requisition form written in duplicate and signed by a responsible person, usually the *chefs de rang* from the food and beverage department. The top copy is retained by the housekeeping department and the duplicate copy remains in the requisition book. Staff must be aware that the linen stock is an asset of the business and costs a great deal of money, and therefore that there must be no negligence in handling it.

Early morning call sheets

Many guests for one reason or another may ask for an early morning call; they may also request early morning tea, coffee, newspapers or breakfast in their rooms. Requests for an early call would be very important, especially if the guests have aeroplanes or trains to catch or an important business appointment to keep; therefore, it is essential that all staff

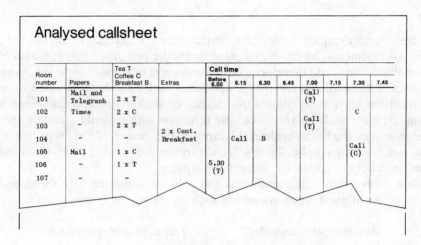

Figure 9.2 *Analysed call sheet*

are made aware of the importance of reporting any such requests made to them personally to the reception office or duty night porters, who are usually responsible for making out the early morning call sheets (Fig. 9.2). Copies of this sheet are distributed to the telephonists and housekeeping department. Either the night staff or the chambermaids serve early morning teas or breakfasts to the bedrooms, either at a set time, or as specified on the call sheet. Using the triplicate checking pad, a copy of the order is made out and given to the stillroom to obtain the tea tray, or in the case of breakfast the copy would go to the kitchen; the second copy of the order goes to the billing or reception office for entry on to the guest's account in the tabular ledger, while the third copy remains on the pad as a record. In large hotels separate call sheets are made out for each floor.

Many modern hotels have now installed early morning tea and coffee facilities in the bedrooms as an alternative to serving early morning teas.

9.2 SPECIAL REQUIREMENTS

It is the responsibility of the reception office to pass on to the correct department any special requests or requirements made by the guest. Details of special diets would be sent on an internal memorandum to the restaurant manager, who would ensure that the *chef de cuisine* and his or her staff were informed.

A request for an extra bed or cot to be placed in a bedroom would be passed on to the head housekeeper who would see that the additional furniture is put into the room and extra linen drawn if necessary.

A guest who wanted his car cleaned or serviced while in residence at the hotel would inform the reception desk and the detailed information would be passed on to the garage attendant for action.

Continuous duplicate stationery is used for this type of internal memorandum to different departments, the top copy going to the department concerned, and the bottom copy being kept for record purposes.

Flowers

Large hotels usually employ florists on a contract basis, who regularly supply and change the floral arrangements. In smaller establishments the receptionist or housekeeper may be responsible for the task; therefore a basic knowledge of floral décor is always an asset.

Flowers and their colours can play a significant part if the hotel is asked to organise special functions such as wedding anniversaries or wedding receptions. When making arrangements for a wedding reception, the reception office should ascertain the colour schemes chosen by the bride, bridesmaids, and other members of the party, and bear this in mind when arranging the flowers for the reception — details of this nature are important and help to create the correct atmosphere.

Wedding anniversaries have traditions and colours associated with them, and these should be borne in mind when organising such an event; for example:

Wedding Anniversaries	*Tradition and Association*
First	Cotton
Second	Paper
Third	Leather
Fourth	Flowers
Fifth	Wood
Sixth	Candy
Seventh	Copper
Eighth	Bronze
Ninth	Pottery
Tenth	Tin
Eleventh	Steel
Twelfth	Linen
Thirteenth	Lace
Fourteenth	Ivory
Fifteenth	Crystal
Twentieth	China
Twenty-fifth	Silver
Thirtieth	Pearl
Thirty-fifth	Coral
Fortieth	Ruby
Forty-fifth	Sapphire
Fiftieth	Gold
Fifty-fifth	Emerald
Sixtieth	Diamond

Notable dates in the calendar

There are certain notable days throughout the year which could mean that the hotel is specially decorated or that functions would be held in the hotel by various clubs and societies. The reception office staff should be aware of these dates and their associations.

Date	Association
1 January	New Year's Day
6 February	Accession of Queen Elizabeth II
14 February	St Valentine's Day
1 March	St David's Day (*daffodils and leeks*)
17 March	St Patrick's Day (*shamrock and green*)
21 April	Birthday of Queen Elizabeth II
23 April	St George's Day (*roses — red and white*)
1 July	Dominion Day (Canada – 1887)
4 July	Independence Day (USA)
14 July	Bastille Day (France)
15 July	St Swithun's Day
28 September	Dominion Day (New Zealand — 1907)
29 September	St Michael's Day (Michaelmas Day)
24 October	United Nations Day
	On or about
11 November	Remembrance Sunday (*poppies*)
30 November	St Andrew's Day (blue — *thistle, heather*)
25 and 26 December	Christmas Day and Boxing Day.

9.3   FIRST AID

Everyone should have a basic knowledge of first aid and be able to render it when necessary, but it should be borne in mind that it is only a temporary measure until a doctor arrives. In cases of serious accidents a doctor or ambulance must be called immediately and the reception desk should have a physicians' list to hand for emergencies. First aid boxes must be provided and staff must be shown the contents and where each box can be located. When it is necessary to render first aid, the basic procedures are set out as follows.

Bleeding

Direct pressure by either the fingers or hand on an open, clean wound will help control the bleeding. Apply a sterile dressing or pad and bandage firmly. Do not apply a tourniquet. If the bleeding is not controlled increase pressure with the hand and apply more pads.

Burns and scalds

If possible, immerse the burn or scald in cold water to alleviate the pain. *Do not* remove any burnt clothing. *Do not* apply any oils or ointments, and do not break any blisters. The burned area should be covered with a dry sterile dressing or some clean fabric. Patients with severe burns should be treated for shock and taken to a hospital or doctor without delay.

Shock

A person in shock is pale, and the skin usually cold and clammy. The pulse is fast and breathing quick and irregular. The patient should be laid down with head low and legs raised slightly, and covered with a blanket or clothing to keep him warm. No stimulants should be given.

Electric shock

If the patient is still in contact with electrical equipment, switch off the electrical supply at once. If this is not possible, do not touch him or her unless protected by rubber gloves or rubber soles on the shoes. Treat as for shock and apply artificial respiration if necessary.

Artificial respiration or resuscitation

If a person has ceased to breathe, immediately lay the person on his or her back. Clear the airway by tilting the head and chin backwards away from the chest. Make sure there is no obstruction by the tongue or foreign matter. Open your mouth, take a deep breath, pinch the casualty's nostrils together, then seal his or her mouth with your lips, keeping the head back all the time, and blow into the lungs until the chest rises. Remove your mouth and watch the chest deflate. Give the first four inflations as rapidly as possible, then repeat this operation as long as is necessary. Remember, time saves lives.

Fainting

Lay the patient down and raise the lower limbs. Loosen tight clothing and ensure fresh air by not allowing people to crowd around the casualty.

The coma position

This is sometimes called the 'recovery position'. If patients are unconscious, turn them on their side in a 'climbing' position (one leg slightly bent), so that if they should vomit they will not choke. Dentures should be removed, and tight clothing loosened.

Nose bleed

Sit the patient up with head slightly forward to prevent blood going down the throat and choking him or her. Pinch the fleshy part of the bridge of the nose. If profuse bleeding continues, call a doctor.

Foreign bodies in the eye

Lifting the upper lid over the lower lid will often bring the foreign body on to the lower lid from whence it can be removed. Blowing the nose will help the eyes to water and wash the object out of the eye. Never rub the eye or use tweezers. If the object is clearly visible, a moistened piece of soft paper can be used to remove it. If the object is embedded in the eyeball, leave it for a doctor to remove.

Choking

This is usually caused by food or some other foreign body obstructing the windpipe. This can be alleviated by getting the patient to bend over and then, with the flat of the hand, thumping between the shoulder blades. A small child can be held upside down and thumped on the back. If this does not help, tickle the back of the throat with the fingertips and try and make the patient vomit or cough. If neither method helps, get medical assistance immediately.

Poisons

If the patient is unconscious, do not attempt to treat except with artificial respiration. Casualties of corrosive poisons such as acids, if they are conscious, should be given quantities of milk to drink. With non-corrosive poisons, including sleeping pills or narcotics, the patient should be made to vomit by touching the back of the throat with the fingertips, or by giving two tablespoonfuls of salt in warm water to drink.

Fractures

Move the patient as little as possible — immobilise and support the injured part. Call a doctor or ambulance. If it is essential to transport the casualty, carefully secure the injured limb to a sound one.

Epilepsy

A person suffering epileptic fits usually falls to the ground, becomes rigid then goes into a fit. It is important that they are prevented from doing injury to themselves.

9.4 ACCIDENTS

Under the Office, Shops and Railway Premises Act 1963, minimum standards of safety and welfare have been made obligatory in premises used as offices, shops, etc., and this includes catering establishments. In addition to the statutory law, all employers have a common law duty to take reasonable care and precautions to prevent any likely harm or injury to staff, residents or guests.

Staff should be aware of the common causes of accidents and if they notice anything that could prove hazardous, it should be reported immediately so that action can be taken to deal with the hazard.

Accident prevention precautions

1. Mats and rugs should be secure.
2. Carpets should be secure and tight, stair carpets in particular — any cuts and tears should be repaired.
3. Floors should be kept in good repair.
4. Gas, electric and open fires should have adequate guards.
5. Any low doorways, projections or unexpected steps should be clearly marked.
6. Dark corridors should be well lit.
7. All equipment should be well maintained.

Accident book

Whenever an accident, no matter how trivial, occurs, it should be recorded in the accident book. These books, in an approved form, can be obtained from HM Stationery Office, and full details of the accident, such as the name and address of the person concerned, an account of the accident and names of any witnesses, should be entered whilst the details are fresh in the mind.

9.5 SAFETY PRECAUTIONS

Fire in the hotel

Instructions for action in case of fire should be prominently displayed in all rooms. Exits must be clearly marked and access to them kept clear and unblocked. All staff must be instructed on the location of fire-fighting equipment and what action must be taken in case of fire or any other such emergency. If fire breaks out, the staff have a definite responsibility for the safety of the guests and, along with the telephone operators, they are charged with notifying all guests in the danger areas to vacate. The basic rules in an emergency are as follows.

1. Report the fire immediately to the switchboard, who will notify the fire brigade. Use fire alarm system if necessary.
2. Switch off lifts and power appliances and close doors and windows.
3. Staff must only undertake fire-fighting if they have been trained.
4. Hotel employees will assist all elderly, sick or infirm persons to the exits.
5. If possible, search all rooms and make sure no one is left behind.
6. The reception staff should remove the register of guests and lists of residents and staff from the building in order that all persons can be accounted for.
7. When the building has been cleared, staff and residents should assemble away from the area and be checked.

Causes of fires

Fires fall into different categories and it is essential that the correct type of extinguishers are used to deal with them.

1. *Class 'A' risk.*
   Fires ignited in paper,.wood, cloth or other types of combustible materials are most effectively controlled by the use of CO_2-water type extinguishers.

2. *Class 'B' risk.*
    Fires caused by flammable liquids such as petrol, fat or oils should be smothered by dry powder foam or carbon dioxide or glass fibre blankets. Water on this type of fire has the effect of spreading the flames.
3. *Class 'C' risk.*
    Fires caused by faulty electrical equipment or wiring must be smothered by using an agent which is a non-conductor of electricity such as the vapourising liquids known as BCF (Bromochlorodifluoromethane) extinguishers. Water or foam will spread this type of fire and increase the danger of electrocution.

9.6 SECURITY PRECAUTIONS

A hotel which is open to the public, guests, residents and staff over a 24-hour period presents many problems of security. It would be almost an impossible task to safeguard property and premises completely. Some hotels instal CCTV (closed circuit television) with cameras installed in the corridors, foyer and public rooms, and monitor screens in a separate area under the scrutiny of the security officer. Commonsense precautions will also help in crime prevention. Officers of the local police will help and advise establishments on security problems and how to deal with suspect parcels and letter bombs, etc.

Residents' property

As the innkeeper has a duty to protect the property of guests, all staff — and in particular the chambermaids — should be instructed on security precautions for the care of residents' property.

1. Any room maintenance required for broken locks, door knobs and sockets should be reported immediately to the housekeeper.
2. If a guest leaves any valuables lying around the room, the chambermaid should report the matter to the housekeeper, who could advise the guest on their safer keeping.
3. It should be emphasised to cleaning staff that it is necessary to lock room doors after cleaning, and if rooms are on the ground floor, windows should be closed or locked if the rooms are empty.
4. All property found in rooms or elsewhere should be handed to the head housekeeper or some other person in authority who will see that it is entered in the lost-and-found book and placed in safe keeping.

Security of premises

1. Staff must quickly familiarise themselves with guests, residents and other members of the staff, and be instructed to question anyone on the premises that they are not familiar with, and whom they consider may be acting in a suspicious manner.
2. Security, portering or housekeeping staff should make regular routine inspections of the buildings, carrying out checks on windows, doors and locks where necessary.
3. Keys and master keys must be under strict supervision at all times.
4. Money and valuables on the premises should be locked away, or under strict surveillance at all times if being handled during the course of business.

5.   Staff must be instructed and made aware of the need of vigilance and security precautions at all times.

Methods of dealing with pilfering

If the management of an establishment have reason to believe that pilfering is taking place, it must be borne in mind that no private person has the right to search another without their consent; to do so would constitute an assault on that person. In order that an employer may have some rights of search, a clause is often incorporated in the contract of employment which states that the employer reserves the right to stop and search employees and the contents of their bags and packages on entering or leaving the premises. If the necessity to conduct a search does arise, the following points should be borne in mind.

1.   The utmost tact and discretion should be applied. It is far better that such an operation is carried out with the co-operation of all employees and people concerned, remembering that unwillingness to be searched may only be because of embarrassment and need not necessarily indicate guilt.
2.   Only persons in authority should have the right to search; there should be always a witness present, and obviously male employees should be searched by a male and female employees by a female.
3.   If any member of staff has been found with stolen property, whether a prosecution is undertaken or not would depend on the circumstances and the policy of the management in such cases, but in any event it should lead to dismissal of the employee, and serve as a deterrent to others who may be tempted to pilfer.

9.7   PROGRESS TEST QUESTIONS

1.   Explain the purpose and use of the 'bed occupancy lists' prepared by the housekeeping department.
2.   As a receptionist on the evening shift, what information would you pass on to the night porter before going off duty?
3.   A guest asks to be called at 6.00 a.m. in order to catch a train to keep a vital business appointment.
     (a)   Explain what action the receptionist must take.
     (b)   The guest is not called until 7.00 a.m., he misses the train, and consequently his business appointment, resulting in financial loss to himself. Who is legally responsible?
          (i)   The receptionist who accepted the request?
          (ii)   The telephonist who failed to call the guest at 6.00 a.m.?
          (iii) The hotel proprietor?
          (iv)   The guest himself?
4.   What colour flowers or special decoration would you consider most suitable if you had received reservations from guests who were celebrating the following wedding anniversaries?
     (a)   Seventh
     (b)   Fifteenth
     (c)   Twenty-fifth

    (d)   Thirty-fifth

    (e)   Fortieth

    (f)   Fiftieth.

5. Describe briefly the action you would take in the following circumstances.

    (a)   A guest receives a minor burn on the hand.

    (b)   A lady falls down in a faint at the reception desk.

    (c)   An electrician working in the section on repairs receives a mild electric shock.

    (d)   A small child starts choking on a piece of food in the restaurant.

6. What type of fire extinguisher would you use for the following types of fire?

    (a)   A fire is caused by faulty electrical equipment.

    (b)   A pan of oil catches fire.

    (c)   A wastebasket full of paper catches fire.

7. The hotel has to be evacuated because of fire. If it is possible, what information or records should the receptionist endeavour to bring out to pass on to the fire officer in charge?

8. A very agitated guest reports that a valuable wrist watch is missing from her room. Describe what action the receptionist should take.

9. Special functions have been booked on the following dates. What do you associate with these dates? Recommend what flowers or extras you would incorporate in the arrangements.

1 March, 17 March, 23 April, 30 November

Appendices

A.1 THE INTERNATIONAL HOTEL TELEGRAPH CODE

The international telegraph code for reserving accommodation is used by hotels throughout the world. One word is used instead of several; it is cheaper and any language problems are overcome.

Number of rooms, beds

ALBA	1 room with 1 bed
ALDUA	1 room with 1 large bed
ARAB	1 room with 2 beds
ABEC	1 room with 3 beds
BELAB	2 rooms with 1 bed each
BIRAC	2 rooms with 2+1 beds, i.e. 3 beds
BONAD	2 rooms with 2 beds each
CIROC	3 rooms with 1 bed each
CARID	3 rooms with 2+1+1 beds, i.e. 4 beds
CALDE	3 rooms with 2+2+1 beds, i.e. 5 beds
CADUF	3 rooms with 2 beds each
DANID	4 rooms with 1 bed each
DIROH	4 rooms with 2 beds each
EMBLE	5 rooms with 1 bed each
ERCAJ	5 rooms with 2 beds each
FELAF	6 rooms with 1 bed each
FERAL	6 rooms with 2 beds each

Additional amenities

KIND	Child's bed
SAL	Sitting room
BAT	Private bathroom
SERV	Servant's room
BELVU	Room with good view
INTER	Room facing courtyard
TRANQ	Room very quiet
ORDIN	Room without running water
BEST	Quality of room — good

PLAIN   Quality of room — simple
BOX   Private garage for 1 motor car
GARAG   Ordinary garage for 1 motor car

Length of stay

PASS   Length of stay — 1 night
STOP   Length of stay — several days

Arrival procedure

AERO   Meet at airport
AEROZ   Meet terminal bus from airport
QUAI   Meet at dockside
TRAIN   Meet at station

Times of arrival

POWYNS This morning
POZUM   This afternoon
RAMYK   This evening
RAZEM   Tonight
ANUL   Cancel rooms

	Morning	*Afternoon*	*Evening*	*Night*
Sunday	POBAB	POLYP	RABAL	RANUV
Monday	POCUN	POMEL	RACEX	RAPIN
Tuesday	PODYL	PONOW	RADOK	RAQAF
Wednesday	POGOK	POPUF	RAFYG	RATYZ
Thursday	POHIX	PORIK	RAGUB	RAVUP
Friday	POJAW	POSEV	RAHIV	RAWOW
Saturday	POKUZ	POVAH	RAJOD	RAXAB

A.2   DECORATIONS AND QUALIFICATIONS

These appear after a person's name in the following order:
Orders and Decorations (VC — Victoria Cross — precedes every other decoration)
University Degrees (substantive before honorary)
Professional qualifications
Honours and Distinctions (e.g. JP — Justice of the Peace)

ACA Associate of the Institute of Chartered Accountants

ACCA Associate of the Association of Certified Accountants

ACIS Associate of the Institute of Chartered Secretaries and Administrators

ADC Aide-de-Camp

AF Admiral of the Fleet

AIAA Architect Member of the Incorporated Association of Architects and Surveyors

AMICE Associate Member of Institution of Civil Engineers

ARIBA Associate of Royal Institute of British Architects

ARICS Professional Associate, Royal Institution of Chartered Surveyors

BA Bachelor of Arts

B Eng Bachelor of Engineering

BLL Bachelor of Laws

BSc. Bachelor of Science

Bt Baronet

CB Companion of the Order of the Bath

CBE Commander of the Order of the British Empire

Ch B. Bachelor of Surgery

CH Companion of Honour

C-in-C. Commander-in-Chief

CJ Chief Justice

Comdt Commandant

Comm. Commander

Cpl Corporal

DBE Dame Commander Order of the British Empire

DD Doctor of Divinity

D Eng. Doctor of Engineering

DFC Distinguished Flying Cross

D Litt. Doctor of Literature

D Phil. Doctor of Philosophy

DSC Distinguished Service Cross

DSc. Doctor of Science

DSM Distinguished Service Medal

DSO Companion of Distinguished Service Order

FAA Fleet Air Arm

FBA Fellow, British Academy

FCA Fellow, Institute of Chartered Accountants

FCIS Fellow, Institute of Chartered Secretaries and Administrators

FRAM Fellow, Royal Academy of Music

FRCM Fellow, Royal College of Music

FRCS Fellow of Royal College of Surgeons

FRGS Fellow, Royal Geographical Society

FRIBA Fellow, Royal Institute of British Architects

FRICS Fellow, Royal Institution of Chartered Surveyors

FRS Fellow of Royal Society

GBE Knight (*or* Dame) Grand Cross, Order of the British Empire

GC George Cross

GCB Knight Grand Cross of the Bath

GCVO Knight (*or* Dame) Grand Cross of the Royal Victorian Order

GM George Medal

HE His Excellency

HM Her Majesty

Hon. Honourable; honorary

HRH His *or* Her Royal Highness

J (JJ) Justice (Justices)

JP Justice of the Peace

KB Knight Bachelor, Knight of the Bath

KBE Knight Commander Order of the British Empire

KCB Knight Commander of the Bath

KG Knight of the Order of the Garter

Kt. *or* Knt. Knight

LCJ Lord Chief Justice

LJ Lord Justice

LLD Doctor of Laws

M Monsieur

MA Master of Arts

MB Bachelor of Medicine

MBE Member Order of the British Empire

MC Military Cross

MD Doctor of Medicine

M Eng. Master of Engineering

Mlle Mademoiselle (Miss)

MM Military Medal

Mme Madame

Mgr Monsignor (Roman Catholic Bishop)

MP Member of Parliament

MR Master of the Rolls

MRCP Member, Royal College of Physicians

MRCS Member, Royal College of Surgeons

MSc. Master of Science

MVO Member, Royal Victoria Order

OBE Officer, Order of the British Empire

OM Order of Merit

PC Privy Councillor

QC Queen's Counsel

RA Royal Academician, Rear Admiral

Rt Hon. Right Honourable

Ph.D Doctor of Philosophy

Rt Rev. Right Reverend

SRN State Registered Nurse

VC Victoria Cross

Ven. Venerable (Archdeacon)

Vice-Adm. Vice Admiral

A.3 MODES OF ADDRESS

Royalty

Title	How to address them in speech	How to address them in a letter	Complimentary close	Envelope
The Queen	Your Majesty *then* Ma'am	May It Please Your Majesty *(formal)* or Madam	I have the Honour to remain, Madam, Your Majesty's most humble and Obedient Servant	To the Queen's Most Excellent Majesty *(formal)* or To Her Majesty the Queen
The Queen Mother	(same)	(same)	(same)	To Her Majesty Queen Elizabeth the Queen Mother
Duke of Edinburgh Princes, Princesses, Dukes and Duchesses of Royal Blood	Your Royal Highness *then* Sir *or* Madam	Sir or Madam	I have the Honour to be, Sir (or Madam), Your Royal Highness's most humble and Obedient Servant	To His (or Her) Royal Highness the Prince (or Princess) . . . To His (or Her) Royal Highness the Duke (or Duchess) of . . .

Peerage — 5 grades

Title	How to address them in speech	How to address them in a letter	Complimentary close	Envelope
1 Dukes and Duchesses	Your Grace	1 My Lord Duke Madam	I remain, Your Grace's most Obedient Servant	His (or Her) Grace the Duke (or Duchess) of . . .
2 Marquess and Marchioness	Lord *or* Lady . . .	2 My Lord Marquess or My Lord Madam *(formal)* Dear Lord or Lady . . . *(informal)*	I have the Honour to be, Your Lordship's (or Ladyship's) obedient servant	The Most Hon. the Marquess (Marchioness) of . . .
3 Earls and Countesses	(same)	3 (same)	I have the Honour to remain, Your Lordship's (or Ladyship's) obedient servant *(formal)* or Yours sincerely or very truly	The Earl of . . . The Countess of . . .
4 Viscounts and Viscountesses	(same)	4 My Lord, or Madam, *(formal)* Dear Lord or Lady . . . *(informal)*	(same)	The Right Hon. The Viscount (The Viscountess) . . . j *(formal)* The Viscount (Viscountess) . . . *(informal)*
5 Barons and Baronesses	(same)	5 (same)	I have the honour to be, Your Lordship's (or Ladyship's) obedient servant *(formal)* Yours sincerely, *(informal)*	The Right Hon. Lord (or Lady) . . . *(formal)* The Lord (or Lady) . . . *(informal)*

Title	How to address them in speech	How to address them in a letter	Complimentary close	Envelope
Baronet	Sir *and* (Christian name) *(formal)*	Sir *or* Madam *(formal)*	I have the honour to remain, Your Lordship's (*or* Ladyship's) obedient servant *(formal)*	Sir . . ., Bt.
Baronet's wife	Lady *and* (Surname) *(informal)*	Dear Sir . . . *(informal)* Dear Lady . . . *(formal)*	Yours faithfully or sincerely *(informal)*	Lady . . .
Knight and wife	(*same*)	(*same*)	(*same*)	Sir . . .
Dame	Dame *and* (Christian name)	Dear Madam *(formal)* Dear Dame . . .	I beg to remain, Your obedient servant *(formal)*	Lady . . . To Dame . . . GBE or DBE,
Government services			**Government services**	
Ambassadors	Your Excellency *or* Sir	My Lord (*or* Sir) *(formal)* Dear Mr . . . (*or* Sir)	I have the honour to be, my Lord (*or* Sir), Your Excellency's most humble and obedient servant *(formal)* Yours sincerely, *(informal)*	His Excellency Mr (*or* Sir) . . .
High Commissioners	Your Excellency *or* Sir	Your Excellency *(formal)* My dear High Commissioner *(informal)*	I have the honour to be, Your Excellency's obedient servant Believe me, My Dear High Commissioner, Yours sincerely,	His Excellency Mr . . . (*or* Sir, *or* The Right Honourable)
Cabinet Minister/Privy Councillor	Minister/Sir *or* Madam	Sir (*or* Dear Sir) *(formal)* Dear Mr . . . *(informal)*	I have the honour to be, Sir (*or* Dear Sir), *(formal)* Yours faithfully, Yours sincerely, *(informal)*	The Right Hon . . .
Citizen's husband	Sir *(formal)* Mr . . . *(informal)*	Sir *or* Dear Sir Dear Mr . . .	Yours faithfully, Yours sincerely,	Mr . . . *or* J. Brown, Esq.
wife	Madam *(formal)* Mrs . . . *(informal)*	Madam, Dear Madam, Dear Mrs . . .	Yours faithfully, Yours sincerely	Mrs . . .
son	Master (*or* Christian name and surname)	Dear Master . . .	Yours faithfully	Master J. Brown (Jun.)
daughter	Miss . . .	Dear Miss . . .	Yours sincerely,	Miss . . .
Professors	Professor . . .	Dear Sir, Dear Professor . . .	I am, dear Sir, Your obedient servant *(formal)* Believe me, Yours sincerely *(informal)*	Professor . . .
Doctors	Doctor . . .	Dear Dr	Yours faithfully, Yours sincerely,	Dr R. S. Stewart *or* R. S. Stewart, M.D.,

Title	*How to address them in speech*	*How to address them in a letter*	*Complimentary close*	*Envelope*
Church			**Church**	
Archbishop	Your Grace	My Lord Archbishop *or* Your Grace *(formal)* My dear Lord Archbishop *or* Dear Lord Archbishop *or* My dear Archbishop	I have the honour to remain, my Lord Archbishop, Your Grace's devoted and obedient servant *(formal)* Yours sincerely,	The Most Reverend The Lord Archbishop of . . .
Bishop	My Lord *and* His Lordship	My Lord, *or* My Lord Bishop *(formal)* My Dear Lord Bishop, *or* Dear Lord Bishop *or* Dear Bishop *(informal)*	I have the honour to remain, Your Lordship's obedient servant *(formal)* Yours sincerely *(or* very truly*)* *(informal)*	The Right Revd. The Lord Bishop of . . .
Dean	(Mr) Dean	Very Revd. Sir, *(formal)* Dear Mr Dean *or* Dear Dean *(informal)*	I have the honour to remain, Very Revd. Sir, Your obedient servant *(formal)* Yours sincerely *(informal)*	The Very Revd. The dean of . . . . *(formal)*
Canon	Canon . . .	Reverend Sir *(formal)* Dear Canon . . . *(informal)*	I have the honour to remain, Reverend Sir, Your obedient servant *(formal)* Yours sincerely,	The Revd. Canon . . .
Vicar/Rector	Vicar *or* Rector *or* Mr . . .	Reverend Sir, *or* Sir *(formal)* Dear Mr Smith, *or* Dear Rector (or Vicar) *(informal)*	I beg to remain, Reverend Sir *(or* Sir*)* Your obedient servant *(formal)* Yours sincerely *(or* very truly*)*,	The Revd. . . . .
Services			**Services**	
Navy Admiral	Admiral . . .	Sir *(formal)* Dear Admiral . . . *or* Dear Admiral *(informal)*	*Navy* I have the honour to remain, Sir, *(formal)* Your obedient servant, Yours sincerely,	Admiral of The Fleet Lord . . . .
Commodore	Commodore . . .	Sir, *(formal)* Dear Commodore . . . *(informal)*	I have the honour to be, Sir, *(formal)* Your obedient servant Yours sincerely,	Commodore . . .
Captain	Captain . . .	Sir, *(formal)* Dear Captain . . . *(informal)*	*(same)*	Captain . . ., RN

Title	How to address them in speech	How to address them in a letter	Complimentary close	Envelope
Commanders	Commander . . .	Sir, (formal) / Dear Commander . . . (informal)	I have the honour to be, Sir, Your obedient servant (formal) / Yours sincerely,	Commander . . ., RN
Lieutenants	Lieutenant . . .	Sir, (formal) / Dear Lieutenant . . . (informal)	(same)	Lieut. . . ., RN
Army Field Marshal	Field Marshal . . .	Sir, (formal) / Dear Field Marshal . . . (informal)	*Army* I have the honour to be, Sir, Your obedient servant (formal) / Yours sincerely,	Field Marshal (Lord) (or any other title) . . .
General	General . . .	Sir, (formal) / Dear General . . . (informal)	(same)	General . . .
Brigadier	Brigadier . . .	Sir, (formal) / Dear Brigadier . . . (informal)	(same)	Brigadier . . .
Colonels	Colonel . . .	Sir, (formal) / Dear Colonel (informal)	(same)	Colonel . . .
Lieutenant-Colonels	Colonel . . .	Sir, (formal) / Dear Colonel . . . (informal)	(same)	Lieut. Colonel . . .
Majors and Captains	Major . . . or Captain . . .	Sir, (formal) / Dear Major (or Captain) . . . (informal)	(same)	Major (or Captain) . . .
Royal Air Force Marshal of the Royal Air Force	Marshal . . .	Sir, (formal) / Dear Marshal . . . (informal)	*Royal Air Force* I have the honour to be, Sir, Your obedient servant (formal) / Yours sincerely,	Marshal . . .
Air Chief Marshal	Air Chief Marshal . . .	Sir, (formal) / Dear Air Chief Marshal . . . (informal)	(same)	Air Chief Marshal . . .
Air Marshal	Air Marshal . . .	Sir, (formal) / Dear Air Marshal . . . (informal)	(same)	Air Marshal . . .
Air Vice-Marshal	Air Vice-Marshal . . .	Sir, (formal) / Dear Air Vice-Marshal . . . (informal)	(same)	Air Vice-Marshall . . .

Title	How to address them in speech	How to address them in a letter	Complimentary close	Envelope
Wing Commanders	Wing Commander . . .	Sir, *(formal)* Dear Wing Commander *(informal)*	*(same)*	Wing Commander . . .
Squadron Leaders	Squadron Leader . . .	Sir, *(formal)* Dear Squadron Leader . . . *(informal)*	*(same)*	Squadron Leader . . .
Flight Lieutenants	Flight Lieutenant . . .	Sir, *(formal)* Dear Flight Lieutenant . . . *(informal)*	*(formal)(same)*	Flight Lieutenant . . .
Flying Officers	Flying Officer . . .	Sir, *(formal)* Dear Flying Officer . . . *(informal)*	*(same)*	Flying Officer . . .
Civil Lord Chief Justice	*(If he is a peer — address accordingly)* My Lord or Your Lordship	My Lord or Sir	*Civil* I have the honour to be, my Lord *(or* Sir) Your obedient servant,	The Right Hon. The Lord Chief Justice of England
High Court Judges	My Lord or Your Lordship . . . or Sir	Dear Judge or Sir	*(same)*	The Hon. Mr (or Sir) Justice . . .
Judges of County or	Judge or Judge . . . or Sir	Dear Judge or Sir	*(same)*	His Honour Judge . . .
Aldermen	Mr Alderman or Mrs Alderman	Dear Sir (or Madam) *(formal)* Dear Mr Alderman, or Dear Mr Alderman . . . *(informal)*	Yours faithfully, *or* Yours sincerely,	Mr Alderman
Lord Mayors *(and Lady Mayoresses)*	My Lord *(and My Lady)* or Mr Mayor or Your Worship . . . *(formal)*	My Lord or My Lady or Sir, *(informal)* Dear Mr Mayor	Yours faithfully, *or* Yours sincerely,	The Right Hon. The Lord Mayor of (London, Bristol, York, Belfast, Cardiff, Dublin and 6 Australian cities) The Right Worshipful, Lord Mayor (all other cities)
Mayors	Mr Mayor or Your Worship	Dear Mr Mayor or Sir	*(same)*	His Worship the Mayor

A.4   THE HOTEL AND CATERING INDUSTRY

HCIMA	The Hotel Catering and Institutional Management Association
AHCIMA	Associate of the Hotel Catering and Institutional Management Association
FHICMA	Fellow of the Hotel Catering and Institutional Management Association
LHICMA	Licentiate of the Hotel Catering and Institutional Management Association
MHCIMA	Member of the Hotel Catering and Institutional Management Association
HCITB	Hotel and Catering Industry Training Board
BHRCA	British Hotels, Restaurants and Caterers Association
ICA	Industrial Catering Association
ETAC	Education Training Advisory Council
CFA	Cookery and Food Association
IHA	International Hotel Association
LTB	London Tourist Board
ETB	English Tourist Board
STB	Scottish Tourist Board
WTB	Wales Tourist Board
BTA	British Tourist Authority
THF	Trusthouse Forte
HTN	Hotel Television Network

A.5   ENGLISH COUNTY NAMES ABBREVIATED

Where no abbreviation is given, names should be written in full.

Avon		Leicestershire	Leics.
Bedfordshire	Beds.	Lincolnshire	Lincs.
Berkshire	Berks.	Greater London	
Buckinghamshire	Bucks.	Merseyside	
Cambridgeshire	Cambs.	Norfolk	
Cheshire		Northamptonshire	Northants
Cleveland		Northumberland	
Cornwall		Nottinghamshire	Notts.
Cumbria		Oxfordshire	Oxon.
Derbyshire	Derbys.	Shropshire	
Devonshire	Devon	Somerset	
Dorset		Staffordshire	Staffs.
Durham		Suffolk	
Essex		Surrey	
Gloucestershire	Glos.	Sussex (East & West)	
Greater Manchester		Tyne & Wear	
Hampshire	Hants	Warwickshire	Warwicks.
Hereford &		West Midlands	
Worcestershire		Isle of Wight	IOW
Hertfordshire	Herts.	Wiltshire	Wilts.
Humberside		North Yorkshire	North Yorks.
Kent		South Yorkshire	South Yorks.
Lancashire	Lancs.	West Yorkshire	West Yorks.

A.6 TELEPHONE ALPHABET

Clear enunciation over the telephone is most important; a system of analogy is useful when having to spell words over the telephone:

A Andrew	N Nellie
B Benjamin	O Olive
C Charlie	P Peter
D David	Q Queenie
E Edward	R Robert
F Father	S Sugar
G George	T Tommy
H Harry	U Uncle
I Isaac	V Victor
J Jack	W William
K King	X Xmas
L London	Y Yellow
M Mother	Z Zebra

A.7 MENUS

In many hotels and other catering establishments the reception office has the job of typing and duplicating the menus for the food and beverage departments. Therefore, the receptionist should be familiar with French menu and culinary terms, and capable of typing and duplicating the menus to a high standard.

A.8 FOREIGN LANGUAGES

With travellers from all over the world visiting the country either as tourists or on business, it is considered an asset for a receptionist to have a knowledge of at least one foreign language so that he or she can communicate with overseas visitors and make them feel welcome.

WHITECREST HOTEL
DYKE REGIS
DEVON

Table d'hôte

LUNCHEON MENU

£5.25

✳

Pâté maison
Consommé brunoise

✳✳✳

Poulet sauté chasseur
Épaule d'agneau rôtie

Pommes château
Pommes croquette
Carottes glacées au beurre
Choufleur polonaise

✳

Meringue Chantilly
Gâteau au chocolat

✳✳✳

Café demi-tasse

✳

mardi le 20 mai 198 .

A.1   *Example menu*

Some useful words in other languages

English	French	German	Spanish	Italian
Do you speak English?	Parlez-vous anglais?	Sprechen Sie englisch?	¿Habla Usted inglés?	Parla inglese?
Yes/no	Oui/non	Ja/nein	Si/no	Si/no
Please	S'il vous plaît	Bitte	Por favor	Per favore
Thank you	Merci	Danke (schön)	Gracias	Grazie
Good day, sir (good morning)	Bonjour monsieur	Guten Tag, Herr . . . !	Buenos días, señor	Buon giorno, Signore
Good evening, madam	Bon Soir, madame	Guten Abend, Frau . . . !	Buenos noches, señora	Buona sera, Signora
Ladies	Dames	Damen	Señoras	Signore
Gentlemen	Messieurs, hommes	Herren	Caballeros	Uomini
Today	Aujourd'hui	Heute	Hoy	Oggi
Yesterday	Hier	Gestern	Ayer	Ieri
Tomorrow	Demain	Morgen	Mañana	Domani
Goodbye	Au revoir	Auf Wiedersehen	¡Hasta la vista!	Arrivederci
How much . . . ?	Combien . . . ?	Wieviel . . . ?	¿Cuanto . . . ?	Quanto . . . ?
Service included	Service compris	Bedienung einbegriffen	Servicio incluído	Servizio compresso

A.9   THE METRIC SYSTEM

The metric system is a decimal system; each denomination is one tenth of the one above it and ten times the one below it.

The gram is the unit of weight
1 kilogram (kg) = 1000 gram (or 10 hg)
1 hectogram (hg) = 100 gram (or 10 dag)
1 decagram (dag) = 10 grammes
1 decigram (dg) = 1/10 or 0.1 gram
1 centigram (cg) = 1/100 or 0.01 gram
1 milligram (mg) = 1/1000 or 0.001 gram

The metre is the unit of length
1 kilometre (km) = 1000 metres (or 10 hm)
1 hektametre (hm) = 100 metres (or 10 dam)
1 decametre (dam) = 10 metres
1 decimetre (dm) = 1/10 or 0.1 metre
1 centimetre (cm) = 1/100 or 0.01 metre
1 millimetre (mm) = 1/1000 or 0.001 metre

The litre is the unit of capacity
1 kilolitre (kl) = 1000 litres (or 10 kl)
1 hectolitre (hl) = 100 litres (or 10 dal)
1 decalitre (dal) = 10 litres
1 decilitre (dl) = 1/10 or 0.1 litre
1 centilitre (cl) = 1/100 or 0.01 litre
1 millilitre (ml) = 1/1000 or 0.001 litre

Equivalents
1 litre = 1·76 pints
1 kilogram = 2·2 lb
1 metre = 39·3708 inches
8 kilometres = 5 miles (1 km = 5/8 mile)

Approximate measures
1 lb = ½ kilogram
8 ozs = 240 grams
4 ozs = 120 grams
1 oz = 30 grams
1 gallon = 4½ litres
1 quart = 1⅛ litres
1 pint = ½ litre
½ pint = ¼ litre
¼ pint = ⅛ litre

Index